Praise for *You've Got This!*

Margie is a unique combination of compassion and sophistication, giving her amazing insight and a unique ability to deliver it. Keep the messages of this book ever in your ear, and negative voices in your head will fall away.

— **Marianne Williamson,** Bestselling author and politician

You've Got This! is a high five to the human spirit. It's a full throttle, rallying cry that inspires, entertains, and instructs. Margie's compelling and personal stories reveal fundamental truths about what it takes to make extraordinary things happen in your life. This is a big-hearted, hope-raising, humor-filled book you'll return to whenever you feel doubt, lose confidence, or hit a wall. Keep it handy. I certainly will.

— **Jim Kouzes,** Co-author of *The Leadership Challenge* and Executive Fellow, Leavey School of Business, Santa Clara University

Margie Warrell has written a book so compelling that I already have a list of friends and colleagues — both women and men — with whom I can't wait to share it. She challenges us to move from a fear-based paradigm to a faith-based one — faith in ourselves to overcome even the greatest hurdles and problems. Thank you, Margie, for all you've done to help me!

— **Kathy Calvin,** President and CEO, United Nations Foundation

You've got to get this book! Margie provides an accessible, evidence-based road map for flourishing in the midst of life's challenges.

— **Tal Ben-Shahar,** *New York Times* Bestselling author of *Happier* and Cofounder of Happiness Studies Academy

You've Got This! will help you build confidence and slay self-doubt. I strongly recommend it to anyone wanting to rise stronger, lead better and grow their impact in today's fast moving, ever-changing world.

— **Maya Hari,** Vice President, Twitter Asia Pacific

You've Got This! is packed with hard-won and heart-felt wisdom. If you've ever been afraid that you lack what you need to achieve your highest aspirations, this is the book for you.

— **Ron Kaufman,** *New York Times* Bestselling author
of *Uplifting Service*

Throughout Margie Warrell's adventurous life she's had to reassure herself *'I've got this!'* many times. And don't we all need that too? Now we have a handbook of how to do just that.

— **Jane Wurwand,** Founder, Dermalogica

You've Got This! is a transformative book for today's uncertain times. Inspiring, informative and deeply relevant to anyone who ever struggles to have faith in themselves, it will empower you to unleash your true genius and embrace your challenges with the courage to turn them into something truly magnificent that elevates not just your own life, but the lives of all around you.

— **Dr John Demartini,** Bestselling author of *The Values Factor*
and creator of *The Breakthrough Experience*

You've Got This! will help you decide what you really want and discover within yourself all you need to take the next step.

— **Claire Chiang,** Co-Founder, Banyan Tree Hotels and Resorts

Margie Warrell did it again! This book is full of practical wisdom and profoundly motivating advice that you'll come back to time and time again to be reminded: YOU'VE GOT THIS.

— **Susan Brady,** CEO, Simmons University Institute
for Inclusive Leadership

Margie Warrell is a shining light; just what this century needs. I found myself reading *You've Got This!* with tears and inspiration. There's so much value packed in its pages, that reading it several times may be in order.

— **David Wood,** Coach, Speaker and CEO, PlayforReal

If you want to get out of your own way to evolve into your greatest self, then read this book.

— **Rebecca Heino, PhD**, Professor and Academic Director, Columbia University

Brimming with practical advice, proven strategies and heart-won wisdom, this book will give you the deep confidence and tools you need to stay grounded when the world around you feels shaky.

— **Suzi Pomerantz,** CEO, Innovative Leadership International

If you ever doubt yourself too much and back yourself too little, this book is for you. Written in Margie's down-to-earth yet uplifting style, *You've Got This!* will help you find the courage you need in those moments when it matters most.

— **Emma Isaacs,** Founder and Global CEO, Business Chicks

This book will deepen your trust in your true voice and spirit so you can move past the fears that keep you from living your fullest potential and highest purpose.

— **Warwick Fairfax,** Founder, Crucible Leadership

You've Got This! is simply one of those books that will be read and re-read again. If you're looking to find that bit of courage, Margie's words will inspire you to take the next step.

— **Tami Roos, PhD,** Bestselling author of *Presence to Power*

You've Got This, makes true on its promise to be life-changing. Far more than a book, it's an organic experience you'll reach for again and again to reconnect you to your power. Spoiler alert — You've (already) got this!

— **Theresa M. Robinson,** Author of *The WarriHER's Playbook*

Margie Warrell has done it again. Jammed with humour, stories and wisdom, *You've Got This!* will revolutionise your thinking, unleash your potential and transform your life. The question is, are you ready?

— **Janine Garner,** Entrepreneur and Author of *It's Who You Know*

You've Got This! will help you conquer the negative thinking that prevents you from unleashing the champion within. Margie's authenticity shines through, and her courage-building wisdom leaps off every page. It's time to kick doubt and fear to the curb!

— **Layne Beachley AO,** World champion surfer, Chairperson, Surfing Australia

you've got this!

MARGIE WARRELL

BEST-SELLING AUTHOR OF **TRAIN THE BRAVE,**
STOP PLAYING SAFE AND **MAKE YOUR MARK**

you've got this!

THE LIFE-CHANGING POWER OF
TRUSTING YOURSELF

WILEY

First published in 2020 by John Wiley & Sons Australia, Ltd
42 McDougall St, Milton Qld 4064

Office also in Melbourne

Typeset in Garamond Premier Pro 11.5/14.5pt

© John Wiley & Sons Australia, Ltd 2020

The moral rights of the author have been asserted

ISBN: 978-0-730-36844-1

A catalogue record for this book is available from the National Library of Australia

Cover design: Wiley
Front cover and internal image: © guvendemir/Getty Images
Author photo: Alise Black

Printed in USA by Quad/Graphics

VC17D28FB-D180-4B91-AAFC-8608FFC123E5_012320

Disclaimer

The material in this publication is of the nature of general comment only, and does not represent professional advice. It is not intended to provide specific guidance for particular circumstances and it should not be relied on as the basis for any decision to take action or not take action on any matter which it covers. Readers should obtain professional advice where appropriate, before making any such decision. To the maximum extent permitted by law, the author and publisher disclaim all responsibility and liability to any person, arising directly or indirectly from any person taking or not taking action based on the information in this publication.

CONTENTS

About the author   *xi*
Introduction   *xiii*

THE DARING
1   **Don't Wait for Confidence:** *Begin before you feel ready*   3
2   **Doubt Your Doubts:** *Stop letting fear call the shots*   19
3   **Dial Up Your Daring:** *Be bold in the vision for your life*   37

THE GROWING
4   **Embrace Your Fallibility:** *Get off your own back and forgive your failings!*   57
5   **Strengthen Your Wings:** *Expand your capacity to soar*   77
6   **Use Your Gifts:** *Trust your talents and play to your strengths*   91
7   **Dear Women:** *Stop selling yourself short and talking yourself down*   107
8   **Dear Men:** *Your greatest strength is found in vulnerability*   123

THE BECOMING
9   **Choose Faith Over Fear:** *A greater force has your back*   139
10   **Find Your Uplift:** *Connect to people who help you rise*   153
11   **Surrender Resistance:** *Embrace the struggle and transform yourself*   171
12   **Own Your Power:** *Lead the change you want to see*   189

Acknowledgements   *205*
Index   *209*

ABOUT THE AUTHOR

Margie Warrell has walked the path of courage many times since growing up, the big sister of seven, on a small dairy farm in rural Victoria, Australia.

From backpacking around the world in her early twenties to starting a business with four young children in a new country, Margie has gained valuable insights about defying self-doubt, building resilience and embracing life's challenges with faith instead of fear.

A member of the Advisory Board of Forbes School of Business & Technology, honoree of the Women's Economic Forum and a sought-after international speaker, Margie draws on her diverse background in business, psychology, and coaching to get to the heart of what holds people and organisations back.

The titles of Margie's previous bestselling books — *Find Your Courage, Stop Playing Safe, Train the Brave* and *Make Your Mark* — reflect her passion for unleashing human potential and emboldening people to live more purposeful, courageous lives. Her clients include NASA, Salesforce, Deloitte, Morgan Stanley, SAP, Marriott, United Health, Mars, Johnson & Johnson, MetLife, Berkshire Hathaway and Google.

Margie's ability to share accessible insights and practical advice for thriving amid the pressures and problems of today's world have made her a regular commentator with leading media outlets such as the *Today* show, CNN, CNBC, *Fox & Friends* and Bloomberg. She also hosts the *Live Brave* podcast and her 'Courage Works' column with Forbes has been read by millions.

Margie also enjoys embarrassing her kids by singing too loudly and taking long hikes in beautiful places. Most recently she summitted Mt Kilimanjaro with her husband Andrew and their four teenage children.

More at margiewarrell.com

'As soon as you trust yourself, you will know how to live.'

Johann Wolfgang von Goethe

INTRODUCTION

Sometimes we have to be braver than we want to be.

And sometimes, when our challenges press in and our fears rise up, a little encouragement can make all the difference.

So when I read a quote by Toni Morrison that said that 'if there's a book you want to read, but it hasn't been written yet, then you must write it', I took her words to heart.

This is that book.

It's a book for anyone who needs a little encouragement to trust themselves more deeply and doubt themselves less often.

Whatever circumstances landed this book in your hands, whether by chance of fate or fortune, I'm glad it has. Maybe the title spoke to you or a friend gave it to you. Maybe you stumbled upon it some other way. All I know is that it's no accident that you're reading this now.

This book was inspired by my own life experience. In particular, by the many times I've needed someone to remind me, 'You've got this!' There've been a few in recent years.

Perhaps you're currently deciding whether to take a leap of faith in yourself towards a new endeavour or long-held aspiration. One that excites you but also scares you.

Perhaps you've found yourself in a situation you didn't see coming. One that totally blind-sided you, rocked your world and left you feeling ungrounded, anxious about your future and mired in misgivings.

Or perhaps you've ventured out onto that far limb despite your doubts, but now you're unsure how to navigate the risks ahead, and you find yourself wrangling with fear that your best efforts will be inadequate ... that *you* are inadequate.

I know the feeling. Oh boy, do I know the feeling.

In fact, as I begin this book right now, there is a little voice in the back of my head.

Margie, who do you think you are?

It's a familiar voice, one I've heard countless times. One that has accompanied me on my journey through life. One that, if it had its way, would have kept me from doing pretty much every worthwhile thing I've ever done or might yet attempt.

Like write this book.

I've come to recognise this as the voice of fear. Of course, fear wears a varied wardrobe and appears in many guises. Only sometimes does it present as the acute paralysing fear that gripped my body the time I went to circus school and stood frozen on the high trapeze platform, unable to reach for the bar dangling in the air in front of me, despite intellectually knowing that falling to my death was impossible. Had it not been for my friends below, hands cupped around their mouths, yelling up to me the titles of my books — '*Find your courage*!', '*Stop playing safe*!', '*Train the brave*!' — I might never have taken the leap. (The upside of this experience was confirmation I'd not missed my calling to run off and join Cirque du Soleil.)

No, more often fear creeps into our lives in far subtler and more insidious forms. As excuses. Judgements. Justifications. Procrastination. Distraction. Self-doubt. Pride. Shyness. Busyness. Sometimes even as arrogance, or righteous indignation. Or a sudden and pressing need to go shopping. Or drinking. Or both.

But the effect is the same.

Fear holds us back. In doing so, it shrinks down how we show up in the world. It narrows our thinking, confines our actions and keeps us from doing the very things that would help us discover how much more we could actually do.

Left unchecked, fear leaves us meandering cautiously through life, mired in inertia, polishing our excuses, justifying our inaction. Over time, it chips away at our confidence, clouds our judgement and fractures our faith — in ourselves and in the dreams we once had.

All the while it holds our happiness, our future and our potential hostage.

SELF-TRUST: A DEEP RELIANCE ON ONE'S INNATE CAPACITY TO PURSUE A MEANINGFUL LIFE, MEET ITS CHALLENGES AND GROW FROM THEM.

This book is not just about helping you overcome fear. It's about helping you build faith. Faith in your unique talents and in your ability to pursue the aspirations that light you up, and to rise above the challenges that might otherwise pull you down.

It's also about grounding you in your innate resourcefulness, resilience and capacity for life — for *all* of life, in all its wild, wondrous and messy glory. Emboldening you to trust in yourself so fully that you don't flinch from pursuing the highest vision for your life because you know that the power within you is greater than any problem outside you.

This will take commitment on your part. Not just for the duration of this book, but for the duration of your life. (Sorry, if you were after a quick fix, this ain't one!) After all, your fears aren't something you can defeat once and be done with it ... brave forevermore. Because that's not how life works and that's not what fear does.

Fear is wired into your psychological DNA to keep you safe from danger — or at least what your brain perceives as a potential threat to your sense of security, safety and status — and let's face it ... they aren't hard to find.

In today's climate of fear, we are perpetually bombarded with reasons to feel afraid. Criminal violence. Trade wars. Melting ice-caps. Rising waters. Child predators. Human trafficking. Extremist militants. Cyber attacks. AI domination. Pandemics. Overpopulation.

Those who peddle fear have no shortage of ammunition to fire up your doubts and undermine your confidence to handle what's coming next. Turn on cable news and you'll soon be reminded of the perils of today's world and what happens to those who don't play life super safe. Fear is the most primal and potent emotion which, left unchecked, can swiftly set up residence in our lives and leave us so anxious and cautious that we risk not living fully at all.

Since venturing out from the safety of my parents' dairy farm at the age of eighteen, there have been many times I've second-guessed my ability to handle what might come next. I've had my fair share of heartaches and hardships, struggles and setbacks ... a few of which I'll share in these pages. All have left me, at some point, going nine rounds with my fears, complete with their endless urgings to lower my sights, retreat off that limb and stick closer to home, where it's more cosy, less perilous.

Countless times while raising my four children, I've felt anxious about an uncertain future as my husband Andrew's work moved us around the world. While I tried to find security from sources outside of myself, in the end, the only effective antidote to my anxiety has come from turning inward. From becoming grounded in my own certainty and cultivating a deeper trust in my own abilities to figure life out as it unfolds.

THE POWER WITHIN YOU IS GREATER THAN ANY PROBLEM OUTSIDE YOU.

It's why I embarked on writing this book.

Twice.

The first draft was just for women. Not only because I am one, but because I've had a front row seat in the lives of many women and witnessed how much they struggle with (and are stymied by) self-doubt, false beliefs, mother's guilt and unconscious biases, largely shaped by gendered cultural norms and social conditioning. This draft was going to include much more of my doctoral research into the intersection of gender norms, power and leadership.

But then serendipity intervened. It came in the form of a series of 'up close and personal' experiences with men that challenged my thinking. Outwardly, these highly accomplished men embodied self-assuredness, as though coated with psychological Teflon that I (wrongly) assumed rendered them immune to self-doubt. Yet beyond their masculine 'I've got this' armour, I found a far more vulnerable and less secure side. It brought home to me how much the social norms that hem women in can also stifle men, limiting their emotional freedom and authentic self-expression. Men simply process and react to them differently: less talk, more toughness. And so I returned to first base and began again — this time writing a book for any person who ever struggles to trust fully in themselves, including those whose public persona may radiate self-assurance. I have dedicated a chapter to just men and another to just women, to address the gendered manifestations of self-doubt and vulnerability. (Though whatever your gender, I suspect something in each chapter will resonate.)

So, as I write this now, in a little cabin atop a small hill in a little-known place called Nungurner, I am starting anew on a book for all courage-seekers. (In case you're wondering 'Where on earth is Nungurner?', it's in the south-east corner of Australia, where I spent the first eighteen years of my life, and where I'm currently visiting my parents.) The reality is that male or female, extravert or introvert, wealthy or working class, each of us has the capacity to forge a deeply meaningful life and to evolve into who we are as human beings ... or, as I'll expand on in the pages to come, as 'human becomings'.

It begins with daring to 'trust in our wings' and believe that we can.

However daunting your challenges, audacious your dreams or entrenched your doubts, within you lie the resources to accomplish more than you may have told yourself is possible. Most of all, starting from today, you have the ability to make fresh choices — to *stop* selling yourself short and to *start* living more boldly, deeply grounded in the truth of who you are. Someone who has within them everything they need to deal with every situation outside them.

The inner determines the outer.

Psychologist William James once said that most people live in a restricted circle of their full potential. Certainly, many people never experience the full breadth of their own capabilities or realise their full potential. Fear keeps them living inside the lines, going to their grave with a large gap between the life they did live and what could have been … if only they'd trusted themselves more and been braver.

My intention for this book is to close that gap, or at least to narrow it — to help you build the self-trust required to challenge the beliefs that have hemmed you in (at least until now!); to embolden you to think bigger about what is possible for you, and, when life's storms blow in, to trust in your ability to ride them through with more grace, less angst.

What I've learnt from my fifty years on this planet is that when we dare to step back from the beliefs we've been buying into — to question our assumptions and lean into our vulnerability — a whole new realm of possibilities opens up. Possibilities that can transform our very experience of being alive.

Your future is unwritten. You are the author. If the pages in this book become well-worn and well-read, then I'll be deeply honoured. If not, I will content myself knowing that it found its way into your hands for a short while and trust that it made some impression, however humble.

And in the end, isn't that what matters most? That we do the best we can with what we've been given — to find peace in ourselves and to leave a positive imprint on the canvas of others' lives?

At least I think so.

Learning to trust fully in ourselves is the work of a lifetime. My hope is that this book can help to open your heart and strengthen your spirit along your journey to living a braver, more whole-hearted life.

So here's to rekindling the relationship you have with the highest and deepest parts of yourself.

Here's to you living each day grounded firmly in a foundation of faith — trusting that you are here for a purpose, that every challenge holds a silent invitation to infuse a deeper dimension into your life, and that, no matter what happens, you can handle it.

Most of all, here's to you being braver than you want to be, finding the courage to move towards a future that inspires you, however unnerving, and looking at your reflection in the mirror and fully embodying the words that come out of your mouth when you say, 'You've got this.'

Because you know what? You do.

Let's journey together.

After all, we can be far braver together than we ever can alone.

the
daring

'If I have the belief
that I can do it,
I shall surely acquire
the capacity to
do it even if I may
not have it at the
beginning.'

Mahatma Gandhi

1
Don't Wait for Confidence
Begin before you feel ready

If you've picked up this book then chances are that you're like me, and like so many people I meet in my travels.

You want to live a good life — a life in which you feel fully alive, connected and cared for, and where you're contributing to the world in a meaningful way.

Chances are there are some parts of your life that are tracking along pretty well, and some other parts, well ... not so much. Maybe the ground beneath you feels pretty shaky, or something has rocked your world and left your head spinning and your heart hurting. Or maybe there is nothing particularly wrong, but something just feels amiss ... not quite right, not aligned with the truth of who you are.

Maybe there are some things you'd like to change in your life. Maybe big changes. Big ideas. Dreams so bold that some days they feel more like mere fantasies — about the kind of life you could create if the stars and moon and planets all aligned in your favour.

And yet ... that voice ...

I mean who are little ol' you, with all your shortcomings and inadequacies, flaws and failings, to think that you could do that thing that tugs most at your heart?

To pursue that dream?

To summit that peak?

To build that business?

And so ...

You stick to the path you're on and settle for the life you've got. I mean, it's not *so* bad. (Well, at least not compared to the most miserable situations your imagination can conjure up.)

And you're right, it's not *so* bad as that. It's just not the life you most yearn for ... not the life that sets your soul on fire.

Meanwhile ...

Days pass. Months pass. Years pass. One rolling into another. Then one day this book finds its way into your hands — via a friend, mere happenstance, sheer serendipity, divine providence ... or via a motley pile of unwanted books at a garage sale. (Hey, I'm no J.K. Rowling, I'll take what I can get.)

While I don't know your situation right now, I do know this:

This book has found its way into your hands for a reason.

To remind you of what your wisest, biggest self already knows to be true (yet so desperately needs to be reminded of). And it is this:

That you are here for a purpose.

And for no small purpose, either. And, not only that, that where you are right now is the ideal place for you to learn valuable lessons for what lays ahead. That there are things that you — and only you — can do. Things that will never be done if YOU do not do them. And that, no matter how large the challenges you're facing, or the challenges you'd like to take on, you are capable of more than you think.

Most of all, that every moment of your life up to now has prepared you for the choices you now must make.

You cannot, *must not*, keep waiting until you know what you're doing, until you're sure you can't fail, or until you have the confidence you *think* you need to have, before you get started.

No. No. No.

Here's the problem with that: if you are waiting until you know exactly what you are doing, or until you feel the confidence that you often admire, sometimes envy, in others, then you may be waiting your whole, entire, precious life.

And that will just not do.

Not for you. Not for me. Not for anyone.

The key is as simple as it is scary: begin before you're ready.

THE FASTEST WAY TO BUILD CONFIDENCE IS TO ACT EXACTLY AS YOU WOULD IF YOU HAD IT.

My daughter Maddy is funny (not as in funny weird, but as in funny *haha*). She tells me that I laugh at all her jokes because that's what mothers are supposed to do. But I beg to differ. I laugh because she is comically gifted and exceptionally good at impersonating people, including yours truly. I marvel at how clever she is at poking fun at my idiosyncrasies that, quite frankly, I'd never even realised I had. I might take offence at how well she takes me down, if only I weren't laughing so much.

In her final years of high school Maddy mentioned on several occasions how she would like to try stand-up comedy. I encouraged her to give it a go but she always had a reason why she couldn't. 'I'm bogged down in study.' 'I've got exams.' 'I don't have time.' 'I'm too young.' 'I'm not ready.'

Then she moved to New York for college, to the city that's been the launching pad for many a now-famous comedian. She mentioned it again. I encouraged her again. 'Just give it a go,' I said. 'Don't try to be Seinfeld, just have fun.' Yet again — 'I've got study, exams, too busy, too young, too not-ready' ... *yada yada yada*. Then she mentioned some club where 'newbies' get on stage and get feedback.

'Just bite the bullet,' I said again. 'So what if you're not brilliant? So what if you tank ... though I'm sure you won't. At least you can feel proud that you gave it a go.'

And so off she went to an open-mic night for aspiring comedians.

My phone rang soon afterward.

'OMG Mum, I did it,' her pride and excitement travelling across the 15 000 kilometres between us. 'And you know what, I wasn't that terrible. In fact, for a first timer, I think I actually did okay.'

She then paused for a moment and said, 'Can I tell you something funny?'

'Yep,' I said.

'I made a lot of jokes about you, about how my mum is a motivational speaker and self-help author who tells everyone to be brave and how funny it is how you get all dressed up and put on your whole professional 'got it all together' look for when you get on stage on or do TV or whatever, but how at home you're continually losing your keys, forgetting appointments, or stressing about how you shouldn't have agreed to some dumb dinner because you weren't brave enough to say no.'

'Got to love daughters,' I thought. But then, the twist.

Turns out that the woman at the open mic charged with providing feedback agreed with Maddy that having a mother like me is a rich source for comical material. Then she added, 'But that mother of yours must be pretty good at what does. Because you're nineteen doing stand-up comedy in New York. She deserves a little credit for that.'

COURAGE TO ACT AMID FEAR LAYS AT THE FOUNDATION OF A LIFE WELL LIVED.

I said nothing to Maddy (though I did revel in the moment as I sent out a little psychic hug to that woman). Like teenagers are contractually bound to do, my kids tend to brush off my advice (*yeah yeah Mum, whatever you say Mum*). So it was deliciously sweet to have a complete stranger on the far side of the globe point out to my fabulous yet feisty daughter that maybe some of her mother's advice was worth listening to.

As I have told all my kids over the years (and which they occasionally appear to actually hear), confidence can be overrated. Of course, believing that you are likely to succeed at something has some solid utility. Yet let's face it, confidence can come and go, wax and wane. It's not stable. Which is why courage is ultimately more valuable than confidence. It takes courage to take action despite our misgivings or the fact that the last time we landed flat on our bums and have no guarantee we won't fall short again and make a complete nit of ourselves.

Heck, I'd never have left the bustling metropolis of Nungurner (which doesn't even have a shop ... not one) to move to the genuinely bustling city of Melbourne at eighteen if I had waited until I was confident I could find my way in a wholly unfamiliar new place. Nor would I have bought the world's most uncomfortable budget-priced backpack and set off with a round-the-world air ticket and some travellers cheques three years later. And I certainly would never have ventured onto a stage to speak if I'd waited until I was sure I wouldn't look like an amateur. (I *did* look like an amateur.)

THOSE WHO THRIVE IN LIFE AND EXCEL IN WORK ARE CONSTANTLY BREAKING RANKS WITH COMFORT.

A few years back I had the opportunity to interview Bill Marriott, the legendary hotelier who took the business his father had started as a nine-seat root-beer stand and turned it into the world's largest hotel empire. When I asked him what he'd learnt about confidence, he threw his head back and laughed. 'I've learnt that I don't have as much as people think I have,' he chuckled. 'You get confidence by doing and learning and making mistakes and fixing your mistakes.'

It's true. Confidence isn't built through thinking we're awesome; it's built through action. Martin Seligman, considered the founding father of positive psychology, said that positive self-image by itself doesn't produce anything and cannot be sustained without action. Rather, as Seligman wrote, 'A sustainable sense of security in oneself arises from positive and productive behavior.'

Ask anyone who's ever done anything worthwhile and they'll tell you that it wasn't confidence in their invincibility that fuelled their endeavours. Rather, it was their passionate belief in the importance of what they were doing and their embracing of the risk of not landing the perfect outcome, first time, every time. Their mission exceeded their fear of failing; their 'why' sat in the driver's seat and compelled them to break ranks with their comfort. And so they did. Sometimes it was semi-confident action, sometimes it was knot-in-the-gut nervous action. But always action. As Prime Minister of New Zealand Jacinda Ardern said, 'If you sit and wait to feel like you are the most confident person in the room, you are probably going to be left by yourself.'

When I decided to start running my public Live Brave seminars several years ago, I was not 100 per cent sure that I'd succeed. However, having met thousands of people through the corporate programs I'd run, I had a strong intuition that many people would benefit from a deeper-dive experience to reassess their choices, reconnect with their passion and rewrite their stories. I've now run dozens of Live Brave programs — days, evenings, weekends — and every single time my vulnerability meter has dialled up full tilt in the lead-up to them. *What if not enough people register? What if I publicly humiliate myself? What if people think I'm getting a little too big for my boots with such a bold undertaking?* It may be an Australian thing, or a rural thing, or a female thing, or the whole trifecta, but I feel acutely uncomfortable promoting myself despite intellectually knowing that this is part and parcel of what is required to 'spread the word'. I just wish people could know by osmosis that I was putting on an event or that I was so famous that I could do one online post and, shazam, Beyoncé style: 'Sold Out'. *If only.*

But then I'd be missing the opportunity to walk my own talk, wouldn't I?

And the beautiful thing? By walking my own 'brave talk' it's helped me to help others walk a braver path themselves. People like Brenda, who came along to my first ever Live Brave weekend in Australia. Though only just.

Four days before the weekend Brenda contacted my office to see if she could transfer her spot to someone on the waiting list. I sensed fear was at play, so I gave her a call. 'I've got a lot on,' she told me. 'There's some family issues I need to deal with at the moment, and money is tight and I just feel I shouldn't be heading away for a weekend right now. I've also got a lot on at work' — Brenda worked for a bank — 'and I'm under a lot of pressure. So it's just not a good time.'

Over the course of twenty minutes I helped her reframe the weekend as an opportunity to recharge and expand her capacity to deal with the various challenges she had on her plate.

She agreed to come. Just.

Which turned out to be a very good thing in the scheme of Brenda's life. Because what Brenda had not shared with me during our call was that she had long harboured a dream of launching her own brand of active wear for plus-size women.

'I just have no idea how to even get started,' she said to me during the weekend. 'I don't know the first thing about the rag trade. Zero.' I said to her what I've said to so many women and, in fact, have even said to myself as I've started writing this book:

> *It's okay not to know exactly what you are doing.*
>
> *All that truly matters at this moment in time is that you make this one decision.*
>
> *That you will not just stay where you are.*

That is …

> *You will not wait to be struck by a surge of self-assurance.*
>
> *You will not wait until you get a premonition of future stardom.*

You will not wait until you have the perfect plan or land the perfect conditions.

And you will not wait until you feel boundless confidence before you decide to make a change or take a chance or speak your truth or even simply dust off your dream and share it with someone.

FIRST, CHANGE YOUR BEHAVIOUR, THEN LET YOUR CONFIDENCE CATCH UP. IT WILL.

This might sound like all those fluffy, feel-good, pop self-help platitudes. It's not. In fact, the idea of acting with the confidence you wish you had is backed up by reams of research. William James advised people to 'act as if' over a hundred years ago. More recently, research by social psychologist Timothy Wilson led him to reaffirm Aristotle's approach: 'Do good. Be good.'

If you start changing your behaviours first, it will in turn shift and improve your self-perception and, over time, your confidence. Sticking with what is comfortable may spare you the risk of rejection or failure in the short term, but it doesn't make you more confident; *it makes you less so!* On the flip side, when you act with the confidence you wish you had, you gradually come to feel more confident. Doing something that was once a scary proposition — from delivering a sales pitch to standing behind a podium — becomes less and less daunting and more and more within your wheelhouse.

This aligns with the groundbreaking work of psychologist Albert Bandura, who found our confidence in our ability to succeed at a task (which he called self-efficacy) is based on four core pillars:

1. *previous accomplishments* — past experiences of success and mastery
2. *vicarious experience* — role models, and observing others' success
3. *social persuasion* — positive feedback and encouragement
4. *physiological states* — our emotional reactions, such as anxiety.

So acting with the confidence you wish you had provides you with the experience to sharpen your game, which gets you the positive feedback that counters your doubts. As for role models, maybe you have them. Maybe you don't. But the best place to find them is by putting yourself in the orbit of confident 'can do' people (which you cannot do while sitting at home waiting to feel confident).

Each day you stick to the status quo — waiting to feel fully self-assured, to craft the perfect plan or develop world-class mastery — is a day that you are not taking the very actions that would help you learn and grow and develop the trust in yourself that you already have everything it takes to figure it out.

Because you do!

GROWTH AND COMFORT CAN'T RIDE THE SAME HORSE.

In the year following our weekend together, Brenda rolled up her sleeves and got to work launching her own clothing line — vibrant active wear designed for larger-sized women. She wasn't quite sure what she was doing, of course. She had to ask lots of questions of lots of people. On many occasions she made decisions that, a year later, she would have made differently. Yet only by stepping into the arena, by giving herself permission to start before she knew what she was doing, was she able to learn what truly needed to be done.

Exactly one year after our weekend together, the first shipment of Be Keane Active Wear arrived on Brenda's front doorstep. 'Had I waited until I was confident that I knew exactly what I was doing, my life today would be nothing like what it is,' Brenda told me recently. Not only that, but she'd have missed out on the wildest ride of her life — learning more in the process than she could have imagined. About online retailing. About designs and fabric. About marketing and publicity. But above all, about herself — her gifts, her strength, her power to help other women to embrace the beauty of their bodies.

As I learnt early in life as I mustered up the courage to learn to ride my first horse (who was quite big but very slow), and then later, my second horse, which we won in a raffle (who was totally crazy), 'Growth and comfort can't ride the same horse.' If Brenda had waited until she felt comfortable and confident, she'd still be dreaming about launching her own active wear brand and over 20 000 women in countries around the world (at the latest count) wouldn't be wearing her bright workout gear (myself among them!). And that's not including the men and kids from her newly launched children and men's active wear ranges!

'It was by just jumping in and giving myself permission to figure it out as I went that I gradually began to build my confidence,' Brenda said. 'The only path to pursuing our dreams is to embrace being uncomfortable ... there's just no other way!'

I share Brenda's story because her willingness to take a leap of faith — despite her fears that she'd fall short, lose her money and end up feeling like a fool —lies at the heart of what this book is all about.

Actually, it lies at the heart of what my life is about — helping people like you get out of your own way by rising above the fears and false beliefs that are hemming you in.

Of course, you may not relate to Brenda. Not completely, anyway; chances are your dreams and aspirations are entirely different. (Which is a good thing ... we don't want to crowd the active wear market.) But just imagine how you would feel a year from now, much less five or ten, if you made the decision not to wait another year, or month or week, before making the life-alteringly important decision to just start.

COMPETENCE ALWAYS MATTERS. BUT WITHOUT CONFIDENCE, YOU'LL STAY STUCK IN THE STARTING GATE.

On several occasions over the years I've had people push back when I talk about the importance of taking action before you know exactly what you're doing.

'Surely,' they argue, 'people in positions of power making important decisions when they lack competence is what has gotten us [our country, economy, the world] into such a mess?'

Fair point. You don't have to look far for evidence of this, or for people in high places who have risen well beyond their competency level; people whose over-inflated egos are writing cheques their competence cannot deliver on. Clearly when people are elevated or elected into roles that are beyond their level of competency, and they lack the courage, humility and wisdom to seek the counsel of those who possess it, the consequences of their actions can cause a lot of harm and suffering for others.

So yes, we absolutely need our leaders to be competent — to be proficient in the domains in which they are making decisions, and, where they lack understanding, to seek guidance from those equipped to offer it.

Competence *is* very important. But let's bring this down to where you're at right now. I'm not encouraging you to do a root canal on your five-year-old (unless you're a dentist!) or to set sail around the world if you've never rigged up a yacht. I also doubt anyone is about to offer you the CEO role if you're fresh out of university (unless it's a very small company that your parents own).

WHEN YOU TRUST YOURSELF TO FIGURE IT OUT
AS YOU GO, YOU SPEED UP THE LEARNING CURVE
TO BECOME BETTER, SOONER.

Not knowing exactly what you are doing before you start out or say 'yes' is not about risking the family farm. It *is* about trusting that you can figure it out as you go. As my friend Emma Isaacs, author of *Winging It,* mother of five (and soon to be six!) and all-round entrepreneur-extraordinaire shared with me, 'You figured it out as you went along up to now, so trust that you can keep figuring it out from here.'

A few years back I spoke at a leadership event at Ernst & Young in Sydney. Afterward I interviewed their managing partner, Lynn Kraus, who had taken on the top role a few years before. She shared how she had been asked to take on that role three years earlier but she had turned it down, afraid that she was not yet ready for the role; that she needed more experience and confidence before taking it on.

'What do you know now that you wished you'd known then?' I asked Lynn.

'That I didn't need to wait,' she said. Sure, Lynn had things to learn to be fully competent in such a senior leadership role, but it was only with hindsight that she realised that she already knew a lot, and she had strong support and the wherewithal to figure out what she didn't know.

See a theme here?

To draw on the title of this book, it's about trusting yourself that you can figure it out even when you're not quite sure what the heck you're doing.

That is, you've got this even when you've not quite fully got this ... not *yet*, anyway.

> THE MORE YOU TRUST THAT YOU'VE GOT THIS, THE SOONER YOU ACTUALLY WILL. YOU DON'T BUILD MASTERY BY PONDERING AND PLANNING; YOU BUILD IT BY DARING AND DOING.

Such is the belief of many of the world's most successful leaders, entrepreneurs and trailblazers. Like the one and only Richard Branson, whom I was invited to interview a few years ago (on his private Caribbean island ... it was a tough gig, but what can I say? Someone had to do it!). During our conversations he shared how he'd taken out a second (or was it a third?) mortgage on his family home as he grew the Virgin business. He confided he was never fully sure about what he was doing but he was confident in his ability to figure it out as he went.

> EMBODY CONFIDENCE. HOLD YOURSELF WITH THE SELF-ASSURANCE YOU WANT TO FEEL AND YOUR EMOTIONS WILL TAKE THEIR CUE.

While Richard Branson is clearly an exemplary success story in the world of entrepreneurial risk-taking and trailblazing, his story and those of many others who've accomplished extraordinary things affirms the truth of T. S. Eliot's words that 'Only those who will risk going too far can possibly find out how far one can go.'

So how dost thou do this? Oh, let me count the ways. Starting with that part of yourself you can do the quickest intervention on: your body! As Abraham Lincoln once said, 'Be sure you put your feet in the right place, then stand firm.'

EMBODY SELF-TRUST

Our body, brain and behaviour are all intertwined. Many books dive into the neural machinations of this — just not this one. However, given that your physiology affects your psychology, one of the most immediately effective ways to intervene when your confidence is wavering is to shift your physical state to one that embodies the confidence you wish you had.

Play with me here by doing a very quick experiment.

Take a big deep breath right into the bottom of your belly (where those butterflies tend to run amok). As you follow your breath flowing in and out, imagine yourself feeling incredibly self-assured. As though you absolutely know, without one shred of doubt, that you have totally got this covered and have absolutely no reason to think otherwise.

Now, shift your posture, your facial expression, your shoulders, and pretty much everything about your physical self to align with this and portray a level of supreme self-belief. Like you're Serena Williams about to make her first serve at a charity tennis match. There's no pressure. You're just fully in your power.

How would you hold yourself? Tall. Strong. Chin up. Shoulders back. A quiet, self-assured smile on your face and your feet firmly grounded beneath you.

Breathe into the feeling.

Neuropsychologists have found that even something as simple as gently smiling, standing tall and holding ourselves as though we feel like a million bucks fires off little signals that tell our brain that we're in control and on top of whatever we're facing (i.e. that 'we've got this!'). Sure, you may not dissolve all those butterflies in your belly, but by shifting how you're holding yourself you'll get them lining up in formation.

It's also useful to shift your interpretation of the physical sensations that often accompany stress. Wendy Mendes, a psychologist from the University of California, found that by interpreting feelings of stress in the body as a sign that we're up for the challenge instead of signs that we're under threat, it helps avoid the negative manifestations of stress (such as constricting blood vessels) and triggers positive physical responses that enable us to make better decisions, be more focused and strengthen our performance under pressure. So next time you feel your stomach knot, don't tell yourself 'See, I'm just not up for this' but rather, 'I'm clearly excited and primed to meet this challenge!'

STOP OVERTHINKING IT AND START DOING IT. ACTION IS THE MOST POTENT ANTIDOTE TO FEAR.

So if you've been procrastinating, waiting for a bolt of confidence to strike you from the heavens before taking that leap, it's time to stop. Act like you've already got it — take a leap of self-trust over a chasm of self-doubt and just do it.

And those knowledge gaps? Trust yourself that you'll fill them in as you need to. And if you do stumble? Trust yourself that you'll learn some valuable lessons and be better off for them. Like all the trailblazers who've gone before you.

I know you're able. You know you're able. The question is: are you willing?

Say yes.

Because if not now, then when?

And if not you, then who?

There are things that you, and only you, can do. Things that will never be done if you do not do them.

Waiting until you know you can't fail, until you've banished every shred of doubt and overcome every misgiving, will exact a very steep toll on you. Perhaps even steeper than you can currently appreciate or that you want to admit to yourself.

It will cost you your dreams. It will waste your talents. It will short change you of the opportunity to grow, give and thrive in whole new ways.

And it will deprive all those who would look up to you for inspiration of the example you could have set.

But the biggest cost of all? Your chance of ever knowing how incredibly capable, uniquely talented and awesomely adequate you *already* are. In the words of Anaïs Nin, 'And the day came when the risk to remain tight in a bud was more painful than the risk it took to blossom.'

This is that day.

'All battles are
first won,
or lost,
in the mind.'

Joan of Arc

2

Doubt Your Doubts
Stop letting fear call the shots

In North Korea every household must have a radio mounted on a main wall in their living room. This radio has only one channel, and it's dedicated to government propaganda. The volume can be turned up or turned down, but it can never be turned off.

It's impossible to imagine the everyday life of ordinary North Koreans — afraid to speak against the government for fear they and two generations of their family will be sent to the notorious 'reeducation' camps. Or worse. It's also impossible to imagine the full psychological impact of being bombarded with propaganda 24/7 without access to *any* other information sources.

Yet an intrinsic part of the human experience is to live with our own internal radio channel spurting out all array of fear-laden falsehoods into our mental airways, day and night. Our very own Radio DoubtFM. Left uncensored, its fearmongering propaganda can subdue us into compliant submission so we never dare to speak up or step out for fear of what might happen if we do. Over time, we can grow so accustomed to the noise and negativity that we lose our ability to critically evaluate its dire predictions of the perils that might befall us if we don't play life super safe. It's why so many do.

Of course, we can try all sorts of remedies to shut down that doubt-fuelling discourse. None work. Well, not for long. Which is why we can so easily start buying into our inner rhetoric, treating it as 'the truth' — that we really *aren't* good enough, that it's *not* worth the risk, that now is *not* the time, that it's *futile* to believe it can ever be different; that *we* can ever be different.

You're not that smart. You're not that special. You never will be.

Who do you think you are anyway? And what if you mess up? What if everyone rejects you? You'll look like a fool ... a total loser.

Come on ... just give up, give in and roll over.

It's not worth it ... just give up, pack up and go home.

So we don't pick up the phone and make the call. We don't extend the invitation. We don't speak up, lean in, move on or take the brave leap and say, 'Heck yeah, I'm in!'

Or just the opposite: 'Enough, I'm out!'

LEFT ON FULL VOLUME, OUR DOUBTS CAN BECOME SO NORMALISED THEY KEEP US FROM TAKING THE VERY ACTIONS THAT WOULD PROVE THEM FALSE.

Before I go any further, let me be clear: this book will not permanently eradicate all doubts from your head. Mind you, neither will any other. And I wouldn't want it to anyway. Because self-doubt serves a purpose — to keep you from making impulsive, short-sighted decisions or doing really stupid stuff. Like invest your life savings in a 'get rich quick' pyramid scheme. Or swim across a crocodile-infested river because you lost a bet with your mate. (A guy actually did that a few years back in Australia's Top End. It did not end well.)

Self-doubt can also safeguard us from the lowest inclinations of our nature. In fact, people who don't doubt themselves enough can be downright dangerous. Perhaps a few come to mind: people in positions of power who are so sure of their brilliance and infallibility that they don't pause long enough to question their judgements. Sadly, many leave a wake of destruction and human suffering.

So self-doubt can serve a positive purpose in your life. Many times. Just not at *all* times. The challenge is discerning the doubts that are serving you (the doubts that motivate you to try harder, keep learning or keep you from swimming with crocs) from those that are stifling you — keeping you from taking the very actions that would expand your horizons.

NOT ALL DOUBTS ARE PROTECTING YOU
FROM DANGER. YOUR JOB IS TO WEED OUT
THOSE THAT KEEP YOU LIVING TOO SAFE
AND SETTLING FOR TOO LITTLE.

Over the last century, numerous bright minds have formulated intricate psychological theories of human behaviour and constructs of the mind — such as Freud's id, ego and super-ego — that can be applied to taming our 'inner gremlin', conquering our most primal fears and insecurities, and attaining what Abraham Maslow called 'self-actualisation'. Many have informed my own thinking. However, my experience working with people across many cultures is that the simplest concepts are often the most effective. And one of these simple concepts is that each of us has living within us a 'small self' and a 'true self'. Bear with me here.

Our small self is driven by fear — fear of losing social status, our sense of security or feeling 'better than' those around us. It's all about optimising things that coddle the ego and minimising threats that may chip it. It tends to be petty-minded, insecure, judgemental, defensive, hyper-cautious and prone to negative comparisons, scarcity thinking and, at least for some, compulsive name-dropping. It often enjoys the limelight, but only when it knows it's going to get doused in accolades. Otherwise it's Chicken Little on steroids. It will steer you away from risk every time, even if it means putting you at the greater risk of going to your grave with your song still in you. Because that's how fear works, and that's what doubt does. It is not founded on legitimacy; it is founded on insecurity.

Our true self, however, is grounded in self-trust. It appreciates the risks, but it's not driven by fear of what could go wrong or what you might lose. Rather it's driven by what could go right and what we might gain — how we can *grow* more, *give* more and *become* more. It is the highest evolution of our being.

Our true self knows that who we are is not our past. Nor is it our job title or our bank balance or what anyone might say about us. Rather our true self knows that we are innately worthy and capable of worthy pursuits. It does not focus on probabilities; it dwells in possibilities. It's always available to us as a source of intuitive guidance, grace and grit. However, it doesn't impose its will on us. It just waits quietly for us to tune into it whenever we so choose. The problem is that sometimes DoubtFM is turned up so loudly that we forget.

Now, you may be reading this thinking, 'Yeah yeah yeah, but my small self is a tad more headstrong than most.' You might be convinced that there's something about your unique wiring that makes you doubly prone to second-guessing, self-doubting and fear-casting. And heck, maybe you're right. Maybe your inner Chicken Little is just that bit more chicken than your neighbour's. To which I say, so what? This just means you have twice the opportunities to put it in its place and double the upside when you do!

My friend Jacqui Cooper became an Olympic world champion aerial skier despite the fact that up until she was sixteen she'd never been skiing. In my book that qualifies her for an honorary doctorate in quelling self-doubt. Jacqui told me how she learnt to put up what she called a 'shit shield' to ward off the negative talk — whether it was coming from DoubtFM or her competitors trying to throw her off her game. 'Unless we really pay attention to the self-talk in our heads, it can totally take over. The voices are always going to be there, but you have to make sure your true voice is louder than the false voice of fear.'

That 'true voice' she's talking about — it's your true self.

STAND GUARD AGAINST THE SPIN DOCTOR IN YOUR HEAD, HELL BENT ON CONVINCING YOU THAT THE ONLY SENSIBLE PATH IS CAUTIOUS INACTION.

Which is why you must learn to create your own version of a psychological 'shield' — paying close attention to your thoughts so that, when the voice of your small self starts taking over your mental airways, you can quickly intervene. This takes the form of disputing your doubts (via some questions on the pages that follow) and calling them out for what they are — a bunch of words in your head intent on keeping you planted firmly on the couch, scrolling the social media feeds of everyone else's lives rather than blazing a bold trail in your own.

Let's face it, though: in an era of fake news, discerning truth from fiction can be challenging. Sometimes our small selves can bypass our critical faculties and have us buying into an array of Armageddon-like scenarios to serve their own agenda. Remember 'Y2K' (New Year's Eve 2000 for readers not old enough to remember it), when the world was going to stop turning at the stroke of midnight?

Didn't happen.

It's the same with your small self. It might sound convincing, but it doesn't mean that what it's saying is true. Its words are just ideas, rationalisations, stories, labels and fear-laden thoughts that can turn shadows into monsters and dreams into delusions. They can leave you feeling like a helpless victim of life or a total imposter, a charlatan who could be exposed at any minute.

Some days, it might feel like these doubts are completely overtaking you. It's on those days you have to be all the more vigilant and turn up your internal BS-meter, interrogate your doubts and tune in to the voice of your true self, lest your small self commandeer your life. I've seen it happen many times. I've had it happen a few times too!

THE DOUBTS THAT YOU DON'T OWN WILL OWN YOU.

When you don't own your doubts, those doubts will ultimately own you. So when those doubts start to pipe up — whether in a quiet unsettling whisper or on full blast, it pays to 'interrogate' your doubts with the following questions. Several of these questions are inspired by the work of Byron Katie, author of *Loving What Is*, as well as the latest research findings that have proven the efficacy of disputing our doubts. For instance, a joint study led by Professor Derek Rucker at Northwestern University found that we can reduce self-doubt 'by instilling doubt in one's doubt'.

Can I prove this doubt is true?

Over time, all our thoughts and emotions can become normalised. Like squatters, they can set up permanent residence in your psyche until you don't even question their right to be there. Which is why it pays to step back and take a long hard look at the unquestioned 'truths' you've been buying into about yourself — to give them a little cross-examination.

For instance, can you prove that there really is not one single person on earth who would ever find you attractive, or that absolutely no-one would ever buy your wares, or that you can absolutely never learn to manage money or build a business?

If your doubt would not stand up under cross-examination, it's most likely fake news issued by your small self's propaganda department.

OUR SMALL SELF IS TERRIFIED OF BEING JUDGED AND FOUND WANTING. YET ONLY WHEN YOU DEFY ITS CONSTANT CAUTIONS CAN YOU REALISE JUST HOW CAPABLE YOU TRULY ARE.

What evidence contradicts this doubt?

Our brains are wired with an unconscious bias that makes us hone in on evidence that confirms our existing opinions and discount or deny that which contradicts them. So if you've been buying into some belief about yourself since you were six, when your first grade teacher said you were terrible with math, then you've probably accumulated a lot of evidence for the prosecution. Now's your time to look for evidence for the defence. What evidence can you find from your past or present that contradicts your doubt? If you can find plenty of contradictory evidence, then perhaps your doubt is fear-issued propaganda. Keep in mind the popular acronym for fear — *False Evidence Appearing Real!*

Stand guard against your doubts. Because each time you let a doubt win, you do a disservice to who you are and deprive yourself of the opportunities for building your confidence, competence and capacity for even larger possibilities. Most of all, you lose the chance of realising how little you ever needed to doubt yourself to begin with!

Does this doubt make me feel more powerful and positive?

My basic litmus test for any negative thought that pops into my head is this: 'Is this thought serving me?'

So speak your doubt out loud, tune into how you are feeling and do this little self-audit:

- *Physically.* Do I feel stronger and energised or weaker and tired?

- *Mentally.* Do I feel focused and clear-headed or scattered and overwhelmed?

- *Emotionally.* Does it bolster a sense of optimism and connectedness or amplify pessimism and isolation?

- *Spiritually.* Does it resonate as truth, fuelling a sense of passion and purpose, or does it dim the flame within me?

The most truthful thought can sometimes be the least comfortable. However, if it doesn't leave you feeling anywhere in the ballpark of better or braver, more positive or powerful, then it's likely leaving you feeling smaller and more insecure. In which case, it's not serving your highest good. Just remember, the truth of who you are is very likely not what you've told yourself about who you are.

If you're not sure about saying this doubt out loud, say it with a funny voice. Try your best impersonation of a cartoon character such as Scooby-Doo, Shrek, Marge Simpson or Gollum! This quirky little exercise is pretty effective at helping us dissociate from our doubt and recognise its falsity, if not outright ridiculousness. A woman in one of my programs did this using her best impersonation of Cruella de Vil about not having what it took to advance in her company (a doubt I've come across countless times, more often expressed by women).

'I'm just not good enough to be a managing director,' she repeated a dozen times in Cruella's deep voice. By the end of the exercise she was laughing at herself and realised the unfounded folly of her belief.

DON'T UNDERESTIMATE THE HIDDEN TAX ON YOUR DEEPEST FULFILMENT IN LIFE WHEN YOU LET SELF-DOUBT CALL THE SHOTS.

How is this doubt costing me?

Many times growing up in the Aussie bush I heard people cautioning against risk with the saying 'better the devil you know than the devil you don't'. That is, better to stick with the status quo than to risk the possibility of the unknown. But this is often really, *r-e-a-l-l-y* crappy advice because it fails to account for the opportunity cost of sticking with the 'devil we know' and the misery we bring on ourselves when we do.

Milly is one of my daughter Maddy's closest high school friends. She's clever, quick-witted and tenacious (much like my Maddy!), and our entire family enjoys her company. When Milly moved interstate for university, she quickly set about finding part-time work. She eventually landed a job working in a café several suburbs away from her university accommodation, requiring her to ride her bike into the city, and then catch two buses. In need of the money, she sucked up the commute and always said yes to extra shifts. Over time, her boss became quite reliant on her availability, often asking her to come in early to open the café for 7.30 am which, during the winter months, meant getting up at 6 am to ride her bike in dark, freezing sub-zero temperatures to get there on time.

Despite Milly's work ethic and dependability, her boss rarely expressed appreciation and was often highly critical, making disparaging remarks such as 'You wouldn't last a day in another café', and 'Why are you smiling? You have nothing to smile about.' He'd make fun of her clothing and laugh at the fact she had to ride a bike and catch two buses to work. He told her he had to fire her co-workers for having 'too much fun' at work and warned her that if she spoke to other staff members she'd be fired too. Occasionally when he made a mistake with a customer, he'd blame it on Milly in front of the customer. One time when she was sick her boss threatened if she didn't show up she'd get fired. So she went to work sick. And even on that day, like all others, she never got the break she was legally required to take.

The Milly I knew was always upbeat and cheerful. Yet over this ten month period her confidence took a beating and she began doubting her worth and feeling increasingly anxious. It eventually got so bad that before starting her shift she'd be in tears, anticipating the verbal abuse and humiliation ahead. Each time she considered leaving, her doubts would pipe up and she'd buy into her small self's fears that this job was as good as any she should expect to get. As her boss often told her, she was 'hardly good enough for this one'. Besides, some of her friends had been looking for work for months without success, and the thought that she'd end up jobless for the rest of the year was terrifying. Yet she was hardly having fun outside of work either. As she became more mentally and emotionally exhausted, she grew less social and withdrew from her friends, which ultimately only left her feeling more down. 'Better the devil you know than the devil you don't' thinking ruled the day ... for a while.

Then one brave day, after talking to her family following yet another horrible shift, Milly decided she just had to take the risk and resign. The moment she did a weight lifted off her. But the real magic here ... it took her just one short week to land a new job that not only paid better and had a much shorter commute, but she was now working for people who made her feel really valued. Her new boss often tells her how proud he is of her and how much he appreciates her work. Within a month of being in her new job, Milly was promoted to supervisor and given a range of responsibilities and control that would never have been possible in her previous job.

'I just wish I could've seen earlier the benefits of taking a risk, backing myself and pushing myself out of the hole I was in,' Milly told me. 'Not only could I have spared myself all that misery but I could have had so much more fun with a group of people I enjoy going to work to see.'

Perhaps you've had experiences with a few parallels to Milly's yourself. I sure have. Her 'if only I'd backed myself sooner' sentiment is one I've heard countless times from people who suffered far more, and for far longer, than Milly.

'I was so scared I'd just end up alone and unable to make it on my own,' Kerrie told me after leaving her 22-year marriage.

'After so long with the same company, I just wasn't sure I'd be employable anywhere else,' said Tomas after leaving the company he'd worked at for fourteen years only to land a far better role with a more dynamic, forward-thinking organisation.

BACK YOURSELF MORE; DOUBT YOURSELF LESS. WHAT YOU WANT MOST IS RIDING ON IT.

Needless to say, when we let our doubts dictate our choices, they can exact a steep opportunity cost from every aspect of our lives — our mental and physical health included.

I'll bet you can recall times when your doubts kept you from taking a chance or making a change or having a conversation, only to regret it later. Of course, it's impossible to fully calculate the opportunity price you pay — from the intimacy in your relationships to your job satisfaction to your actual bank balance — when you let doubt call the shots. But don't kid yourself that there's not a price. Just know that doubt keeps us from doing things that would open up all sorts of new doors ... doors we might never even know existed.

Research by VitalSmarts, a corporate training company, found that 80 per cent of workers in the US avoid having important conversations because they have too little confidence and too much doubt. But it begs the question: what issues get left to fester and what opportunities get lost because self-doubt silences the very conversations that might change everything? If you're holding off having a conversation for fear of it being awkward or just messing it up, don't kid yourself that there's not a cost.

The same is true in every domain of your life. Letting your doubts sit in the driver's seat limits the horizon of your future. If you're not sure how, take a moment to fast forward your life, as you might with a movie, and imagine what your future might look like if you keep buying into the doubts that have been limiting you. Is that a future that lights you up? Or is it one that leaves you feeling decidedly ho-hum?

Maybe your doubts aren't keeping you from landing a date with the potential love of your life. But don't discount their hidden toll on your happiness — current and future. If you haven't risked rejection at least eleven times recently, then maybe they are. To quote the old bard: 'Our doubts are traitors and make us lose the good we oft might win by fearing to attempt.'

Who might I be without this doubt?

Vincent van Gogh once said: 'If you hear a voice within you say "You cannot paint," then by all means paint, and that voice will be silenced.' I'm grateful van Gogh defied the voice of his small self and pursued his artistic passion, or the world would have missed out on his creative brilliance. But consider the brilliance and beauty the world does miss out on because too many people like you and me surrender their dreams and talents to the doubting voices in their heads. When doubt reigns, actions go undone, creativity goes unexpressed, strengths stay undeveloped and dreams lay dormant. Everyone is left worse off.

So if you have a doubt that you've been buying into for a long time, then think about who you could be — or what you might do — if you banished your doubt. It will require some serious blue-sky thinking. Be bold and creative as you let your mind wander off into the far reaches of your imagination. What might be possible if you gave yourself the freedom to believe that you can do what most lights you up? If you're picturing someone even remotely better, braver or more authentically connected to others than who you are right now, it's a good sign this doubt needs ditching.

DOUBT WILL NEVER OVERESTIMATE YOUR ABILITIES. IT WILL SELL YOU SHORT EVERY TIME.

Shivaun Brown did this exercise at one of my Live Brave weekend retreats. While Shivaun liked her job in a mid-level management role for a local government authority, she felt increasingly bored and was looking for a new challenge that would develop her latent leadership skills. However, she doubted her abilities to advance and wondered if she should give up and start again in another industry. By the end of the weekend she was clear she was in the right industry and resolved not to give her doubts the power to keep her from pursuing more senior leadership roles with greater influence.

Armed with a goal plan she developed over the weekend, on her first day back at work she decided to act as though she no longer had that doubt and set up a meeting with her boss. Her heart beating through her chest, she sat across from him at his desk and told him she'd like to work towards being a director. To her astonishment he told her he had long seen leadership potential in her and, now that he was aware of her ambitions, asked her to step into an acting director role during his upcoming leave. She left his office walking on air. But what really affirmed the power defying her doubts was that within six months she got the 'promotion of a life time' (her words) and was appointed to a permanent director role.

As Shivaun shared with me recently, 'Not only have I realised how little reason I had to doubt myself, but I am really making a difference in this job. I'm good at it and I'm enjoying it — still evolving, still growing, and loving every minute.' Her experience holds two lessons for anyone whose self-doubt has tempered their ambition:

1. Don't underestimate the cost of letting your doubt limit your daring.
2. Getting what you want is strongly correlated with asking for it.

INHALE SELF-TRUST; EXHALE SELF-DOUBT. REPEAT OFTEN.

What might be a more useful belief for me instead?

Consider what you might do if you told yourself the exact opposite of what you've been telling yourself.

Like maybe that you *do* have what it takes or that you *are* clever/worthy/ talented enough or that you *can* handle it or that you *are* capable of far more than you've allowed yourself to believe ... *up to now!*

Sure, some people (like Milly's boss) may have said and done things that made you doubt yourself. But no-one, with the exception of precisely *not one single person*, is responsible for the power that you give to your doubts from this point on. Not your parents. Not your boss. Not your partner. Not your abusive ex-partner. Not your tyrannical second-grade teacher or the mean girls from middle school. Sure, they may have triggered your doubts and may still be fuelling them. But you, *and only you* are the one who has to buy into them. Therefore you, *and only you*, have the power to buy out of them.

You do that by cross-examining your doubts with the questions I've outlined, and then consciously choosing another belief that might serve you so much more. One that doesn't leave you feeling 'less than' in some way. Less than worthy. Less than capable. Less than deserving. Less than loveable. Less than resourceful enough to figure it out as you go.

You might also want to try the power of affirmations. Words of affirmation are one of the most fundamental love languages Gary Chapman wrote about in his groundbreaking book *The Five Love Languages* — we all crave affirmation and we need validation to function at our best.

Yet one of the most vital sources of affirmation, which is often neglected, comes from within: affirming ourselves. No amount of external praise and appreciation can ever be enough if it's not being matched by how we are internally affirming and appreciating ourselves.

Positive affirmations are positive phrases or statements used to counter and replace unhelpful thoughts and shift how you think, feel and act in your relationships and in the world. They are not about manipulating something outside of yourself. Rather, affirmations speak from, and to, the deepest part of who you are. In doing so, they activate your deepest source of power, enabling you to show up in the world in a different, more grounded way, radiating an energy that attracts what you seek.

While affirmations might sound 'woo woo', numerous empirical studies have proven their efficacy. The most well-known is Self-Affirmation Theory by social psychologist Claude Steele. One study I came upon in the scientific journal *Personality and Social Psychology Bulletin* found that when people spent five minutes writing down, appreciating and affirming their strengths and skills, they performed far better in a negotiation than those who didn't. Likewise, neuroscience research using MRI technology has shown evidence that certain neural pathways are increased when people practise self-affirmation.

In *The Secret Life of the Brain*, Richard Restak describes how three lobes of the brain interact to process and integrate information at a level beyond our conscious awareness: one lobe registers what we speak, another what we hear and the other what we read. So whatever belief you want to build, it is helpful to affirm it using these three modalities. Below are three simple steps to help you do just that. While you might be tempted to brush past this right now, I encourage you to take three minutes and to actually do the steps, not just read them!

Step one: Write down your affirmation in a way that uses a first person *active* voice, in the *present* tense, and states whatever you want in a *positive* way. For instance:

I speak with confidence and surround myself with people who empower me.

I am worthy of my boldest aspirations and attract the ideal people to help me make them reality.

I am exactly where I need to be to take my career/business/life to the next level.

I have faith in my ability to handle my challenges with grace and grit.

I am ready to make the brave decisions that will serve the highest good.

Step two: Stand tall, take a deep breath of self-belief, and say your affirmation out loud ten times. (But before you do, press 'record' on your phone.)

Step three: Still standing tall, your feet grounded firmly in the truth of your greatness, place your hand on your heart and listen to your recording.

Repeat reading, saying and listening to your affirmation at least twice every day until you feel truly grounded in this belief and ready for a new one to level up your life yet again.

There is a school of thought that claims that saying your affirmations in the second person — for example, '[Insert your name here], you are strong, fearless and fabulous!' — is more powerful. I say, do whatever works for you. *Just do something!*

EVERY HUMAN BEING IS CAPABLE OF TAKING ACTIONS THAT WILL MAKE THEM FEEL MORE ALIVE. YOU ARE NO EXCEPTION. OWN YOUR LIFE.

Heck, if I had to be the world's greatest literary phenomenon before I began this book you would not be holding it. But somehow it's found its way into your hands, and hopefully something you've read so far has been helpful. My point: you don't have to have the IQ of Einstein or possess Michelangelo-like mastery to be of value to others and move your life forward.

Don't let your doubt win.

So let me ask you: if I had a magic wand that could permanently remove the doubts that have been holding you back, what action would you take?

Unfortunately, I seem to have misplaced my magic wand. However, the good news is that the power is right there in your shoes, Dorothy. The power to decide whether you're going to let your self-doubts keep you from venturing down whatever yellow brick road lights you up. And each time you take a step down that road — taking action despite your doubts — you weaken the hold they have over you and reinforce the hold you have over yourself.

So let's get specific here. If you were going to reclaim the power you've given your doubts, what would you do? Write it down or say it out loud. Like, right now (you've been putting this off too long already). Here are a few ideas to get you thinking.

Reset your sights on that long held dream you've been afraid to pursue for fear of falling short

Commit to having that courageous conversation you've been putting off for too long

Share that dream. Schedule that action. Stop making excuses and set your alarm

Reach out to that person you'd love to connect (or reconnect) with

Pursue a new role or venture onto a new career path entirely

Step away from a relationship or enter into a new one

Say no. Say yes. Say I love you. Say let's do it!

Set up a meeting with a financial advisor

Start a family or have another child

Brave the possibility of rejection

Take that leap of faith. Finally

Begin writing that book

Make that decision

Attend that event

Book that trip

Shut up shop

Start over

Move on

Lean in

Let go

Just

Do

It

!

Of course, as soon as you commit to defying your doubt, your small self will likely get defensive and double down. So be ready when DoubtFM starts flooding you with all the reasons *why not*.

You're not good enough. They won't like you. You're too young, too old, too busy, too chicken. Besides, it's the wrong time of year.

Tell them *hush up*, tune into your true self and follow its lead.

DOUBT KILLS MORE DREAMS THAN OVER DARING EVER CAN.

You and I have likely never met. But one thing I know about you beyond any shadow of a doubt is this:

When you reclaim the power you've given your doubts and step towards whatever tugs most at your heart, all sorts of magical possibilities will begin to appear for you.

You'll open incredible doors that you had thought were beyond you.

You'll uncover hidden talents and sharpen strengths like never before.

You'll enjoy awesome experiences with exceptional people you'd never have met otherwise.

You'll discover whole new horizons previously hidden beyond your field of vision.

But most of all, you'll discover that you never had to doubt yourself to begin with.

Victor Hugo said that there is nothing more powerful than an idea whose time has come.

Well, I say *your* time has come.

Time to stop selling yourself short and short-changing the world.

Time to stop asking 'Who am I to be amazing, admired, adventurous, inspirational?'

Time to start living into the real question: 'Who am I not to be?'

'Your doubts keep you from putting your arse where you heart is,' wrote Steven Pressfield in *The War of Art*.

So spare yourself arriving at some distant today and wondering who you could have been had you only dared to trust in yourself. Time to put your derriere where your heart is.

'We must dare
and dare again
and go on daring.'

Georges Jacques Danton

3
Dial Up Your Daring
Be bold in the vision for your life

At sixteen, after nearly a decade in Catholic convent schools in Melbourne, my mother decided to enter a religious order to become a nun. After nine years in the convent, just a few months shy of making her final vows, she decided to leave the cloistered world of the convent and started teaching at a Catholic school in the rural town of Sale, in the south-east corner of Australia. Sale just so happens to be an hour's drive from the even more rural place of Nungurner, where my father lived, milking cows on his parents' dairy farm.

To cut a long story short, they met, got married and had seven kids. Francis Patrick came first. Then fast on his heels, yours truly ... Margaret Mary. Followed by Pauline, Stephen, Anne, Peter and Catherine.

My parents assumed traditional gender roles. Dad managed the farm and most jobs outside the home. Mum managed everything inside. My siblings and I largely followed suit. The boys did more of the outside 'boy jobs'. The girls did more of the more domestic, indoor 'girl jobs'. By age ten I could whip up a batch of scones in between preparing baby bottles, washing dishes and folding nappies for my younger siblings. (As soon as one was out of nappies another one would be on the way, and disposables were never a budgetary option.)

Growing up on the farm, my horizons extended little beyond the back paddock. (Which wasn't all that far back.) Yet I sensed there was a whole lot more world out there waiting to be explored and experienced. As my adolescent years ticked along, my yearning to spread my wings grew stronger. The green rolling hills, long pristine beaches, gum-treed bushlands and picturesque countryside had shaped my youth, but I wanted something different for my future. What that was, I wasn't sure. The unknown beckoned.

Yet I would never have described myself as ambitious. Not because I wasn't relatively driven at school, but because 'ambition' was just not a word, or an ideal, that carried any currency in our family. I had no role models or experiences of ambitious people outside of movies or headlines of those 'greedy tycoons' whose blind ambition had been their downfall. If anything, being ambitious would have been discouraged as vain, indulgent or prideful — traits reserved for the over-reaching 'tall poppies' who would ultimately be brought down to earth with a thud.

Then when I was around twelve, I developed my first major 'girl crush' on a television journalist called Jana Wendt and became enamoured with the idea of being one myself, foreign-correspondent style. At the time, Jana was one of Australia's most prominent journalists, gracing TV screens each Sunday night on *60 Minutes*. You might say she was Australia's 1980s version of CNN's Christiane Amanpour, but with a squarer jawline that I used to try to emulate (unsuccessfully). I used to daydream of following in Jana's footsteps — interviewing world leaders, venturing to the frontlines of war zones and natural disasters, revealing injustices, exposing despots and championing just causes ... and walking the red carpet at the odd black tie gala.

I recall an exchange with my mother around this time. Picture this scene in a farmhouse kitchen.

Me at the bench, separating the egg whites from their yolks for a sponge cake: 'I've been thinking, Mum. I'd really like to be a journalist, like a foreign correspondent, like Jana Wendt.'

Mum, standing at the sink, toddler on hip: 'But darling, you don't read the paper. People who are journalists are voracious readers, they read all the newspapers, *every day*. They know what's going on in the world.'

Me (shoulders slumping): 'Oh.'

Cut back to me licking the ladle clean of cake mix (a guilty pleasure to this day). End scene.

It never occurred to me to challenge Mum's logic. In fact, it took about two decades before it occurred to me that we never even got a daily paper. My parents' only newspaper subscriptions were to *The Weekly Times* and *The Advocate*, weekly rags for farmers and Catholics respectively.

Just to be clear, I am not in any way blaming my beautiful and very selfless mother for the fact that I'm not hosting my own show on the ABC or CNN. A few years after this conversation, she spent eight hours driving me to Melbourne and back to sit a cadet journalist entrance exam for *The Age* newspaper. By that point there were seven kids at home, so leaving a horde of kids behind to run feral on the farm was no small undertaking. As it turned out, I never got asked back to do an interview— likely because, as Mum had pointed out, I didn't read the newspaper and was not much of a reader of anything.

Then one day, after I'd gotten over my Jana infatuation, it seemed that my dad would breathe new wind beneath my farm girl wings. Sort of. I cannot recall the exact situation but it was probably just after I'd taken the clothes off the line, changed my youngest sibling's nappy, peeled potatoes for the nine hungry mouths that clambered around our 'dinette' table each night, whipped up dessert (self-saucing butterscotch pudding with fresh cream skimmed straight off the top of the milk jug) and dried the dishes. (Okay maybe I exaggerate a little here ... but not entirely.)

'Margaret Mary,' Dad said proudly, the promise of praise in his tone, 'You are such a capable young woman. I see you doing great things one day ... *great* things.'

'You do?' I replied delightedly, standing taller, images of Margaret Thatcher, Princess Diana and Meryl Streep appearing in my mind ... *Yes, Yes!* I thought. Dad was onto something here! I held my breath ...

'Oh yes,' he said, beaming, 'I see you one day being Sister Margaret Mary, in charge of a convent.'

A nun? *Me*? Are you serious?!

Perhaps Dad saw my shoulders slump. Whatever the reason, he clearly realised he'd missed the mark.

'Actually, no,' he tried to recover, 'I see you doing bigger things than that.'

Alleluia, I thought.

'Oh yes! In fact, I see you becoming *Mother* Margaret Mary, in charge of a whole order of convents.'

That wind under my wings? Gone. Instantly. Princess Diana may have been a bit of a stretch, but a future Mother Teresa? Noble as she was, for me, after living in hand-me-down and thrift-shop clothes my entire childhood, the idea of spending my adulthood in a robe and habit, vowed to chastity and poverty, unable to wear red lippy, left me cold.

I don't in any way want to sound like I'm criticising my parents. They don't deserve it; in fact, they deserve nothing but appreciation and admiration for enduring many difficult years, through devastating droughts, raising seven children with immense love and little money. Particularly me, as I was a cantankerous teen, and probably responsible for at least half the grey hair on their heads. My parents also gave me deep roots, broad wings and a strong faith — all of which have helped me rise above the hardships and heartaches in my years since leaving home as an unworldly, wide-eyed eighteen-year-old (with a bad perm).

My parents' vision for me was limited by the horizons of their own world. They had none of the opportunity I've had in my adult life to see the world through a larger lens. It wasn't that they didn't think I was capable of doing great things (Dad said as much!), but they simply had no sense of all that was actually possible. How could they?

Being the first of anyone in my extended family to attend university was in itself groundbreaking. Yet staying close to home, where the weekend highlight was watching the local football game, was simply not an option I could entertain. Despite the uncertainty, knowing close to no-one and having to live fully independently (as we didn't know the ropes enough to access any student accommodation), the promise of new urban adventures compelled me to leave behind all I'd known up to then. Looking back now I can see that it was a brave thing to do, to move to an unknown city at eighteen, with minimal financial or social support, but a quiet determination to find my way.

After three years of learning to stand on my own two feet, and numerous ups and downs along the way, I graduated with a business degree, majoring in Marketing. (Why Marketing? I thought it sounded interesting and might get me a glamorous job in advertising or the beauty industry where I'd get free make-up. I was pretty 'deep' back then.) However, rather than get a 'real job' like many peers, I moved back home to the country to work two jobs — sorting frozen corn by day, pouring beers by night — to save up for an 'around the world' backpacking adventure. At the time I thought it would be my one and only 'overseas' adventure and pictured myself one day telling my grandkids about 'the time I went to New York and exited the wrong subway station and wandered lost around Harlem'. My own imagination could not have fathomed that I'd one day be regularly flying around the world speaking at conferences, much less that some of my own children would end up studying in New York.

IF SOME WILDLY AUDACIOUS DREAM SPARKS A LIGHT WITHIN YOU, IT'S NO ACCIDENT.

So why have I shared all this with you? (After all, you didn't buy an autobiography!)

First, because too often we let the vision that other people have for us direct and limit our own.

Second, because we sometimes make negative associations with ambition. We spin ourselves a story that being ambitious is distasteful; that it's far more laudable to content oneself with what one already has. Of course, it's important to celebrate where you are right now and unwise (and dangerous) to equate your worth with accolades, but that doesn't mean there's anything inherently wrong, greedy or ignoble with pursuing the boldest aspirations for yourself and your life.

Other times we tell ourselves it's best to 'go with the flow' and see what the universe brings our way. To which I say sure, don't swim upstream. However, if you don't set your sights on any future vision that inspires you, you might end up some place you'd never consciously have chosen.

Third, because on occasion we have to buck others' expectations, defy what they think we 'should' do and risk their disapproval, disappointment or even rejection. (This includes people who may genuinely love us and sincerely believe we're making a terrible mistake.) Yet if disapproval is the price of pursuing whatever most lights you up, so be it. Surely that is a better price to pay than keeping others happy while forfeiting your chance to discover just how uniquely gifted you are. Far too often we give other people's fears, preferences and desires undue sway in our lives. It doesn't serve us *or* them. And it can end in disaster (the experience of my friend Warwick Fairfax, which I recount in chapter 8, is a case in point).

And finally, because in the grand scheme of this wondrous experience we call life, we fail far more from setting our sights on easily attainable goals than we ever do from unleashing our imagination and pursuing our boldest dreams — the ones that excite our socks off. Like being Jana Wendt ... or Mother Teresa. Of course, different strokes for different folks.

I don't say this to set you up for a life of *striving* towards the impossible. Rather I say this to set you up for a lifetime of *thriving* towards the meaningful. Research has found that people who are working towards meaningful goals enjoy a greater sense of wellbeing than those who don't *regardless* of whether they achieve them. It is the very act of pursuing a goal that stretches us that expands our confidence, competence and capacity for larger challenges — both those we choose and those that come our way unbidden. As the French philosopher Michel de Montaigne once wrote, 'Ambition is not the vice of little people.'

IF YOU CAN ACHIEVE YOUR GOALS WITH YOUR EYES CLOSED, YOU'RE SELLING OUT ON ALL YOU COULD BE.

US President Teddy Roosevelt once said that 'by far and away one of life's greatest pleasures is to work hard at work worth doing.' So if you feel a little uneasy using the word 'ambition' in the context of whatever meaningful goals you're working towards, call it your 'work worth doing'.

The most powerful way to view ambition is not through the lens of what we can get from the world (feeding the egocentric needs of our small self) but through the lens of what we can give (aligning with the highest aspirations of our true self).

Now, just to be clear, 'work worth doing' does not exclude being paid well for your efforts, earning a little kudos from your peers or enjoying the various perks of 'success' — however you define it. Heck, I definitely get a buzz when my work is publicly recognised. But if that applause were the only reason I did it then I'd become hostage to the applause, which would, eventually, restrict me to only doing things that I knew would get me more of it (which would count out much of what I do ... like writing this right now!).

So consider your future through the lens of how you can channel your talents, know-how, creativity and connections to make the most meaningful contribution for others. As Kristina Karlsson, founder of Swedish design brand kikki.K shared with me, 'The magic of our dreams is in how they can be a gift for others.'

So let me ask you this:

What goal would you set your sights on if you were to dial up your ambition and pursue the boldest vision for your life?

YOU'RE ON THIS EARTH SO BRIEFLY IN THE LONG MARCH OF TIME. CREATE A VISION FOR YOUR LIFE THAT SETS YOUR HEART ON FIRE.

'I've never underestimated myself,' said Angela Merkel, Chancellor of Germany. 'There's nothing wrong with being ambitious.' Whether you agree with all her decisions, there's no disputing the indelible mark she has made on the world by daring to step into her power with the intention to serve not just the citizens of Germany, but the citizens of the world, particularly those who found themselves without a home and in need of refuge.

The truth is that playing small and settling for less than the life you are capable of doesn't just do a disservice to you; it does a disservice to everyone who spins in your orbit. And if you zoom up high enough, we are all spinning in your orbit!

'But surely,' you say, 'can't you be too ambitious for your own good?' After all, if you take on too bold a goal, you set yourself up for overwhelm and failure. Would it not be smarter to set your sights on what's doable and doesn't exhaust you?

I mean, is it really smart to shoot for the stars when you know the odds are stacked against you?

Of course I'm biased, however I strongly believe that when you set your sights on something that inspires you, it transforms your experience of life itself — however huge or humble your aspirations may seem to anyone else. What Elon Musk or Richard Branson or (insert-other-trailblazing-stargazing-entrepreneur) is doing is *their* business. This is about what inspires YOU. And only you.

Once you've connected with that vision, write it down. (This makes a difference, trust me.) Then break it down into smaller, bite-sized chunks, so you can at least see the first few steps. This is in line with highly scientific advice on the best way to eat an elephant: one bite at a time.

Ultimately, no ambition is ever too big. How would humanity have ever advanced if we didn't sometimes set our sights on ambitions that seemed outlandish, fanciful and even harebrained at the time? Think man on the moon. Think electric light bulb. Think four-minute mile. Think heavier-than-air flying machine (a.k.a. aeroplane). Likewise, it wasn't all that long ago people scoffed at the idea of driverless cars, much less space tourism. Yet a friend of mine has put a deposit down to secure her spot among the first space-blazing tourists when Richard Branson's Virgin Galactic opens for business.

NOTHING WORTH DOING IS ACHIEVED WITH A GUARANTEE OF SUCCESS. IF IT DIDN'T STRETCH YOU, IT WOULDN'T BE WORTH DOING.

Just be mindful that the higher you set your sights, the more purposeful you must be because no worthwhile endeavour comes with a guarantee of success. The more audacious your goal, the higher the hurdles and the greater the risk of falling short when jumping them. Does that mean you should just drop anchor and settle for the security of where you are now?

You know my answer to that. The risks of playing safe are less obvious and immediate, but they are no less real. As Helen Keller once said, 'Avoiding danger is no safer in the long run than outright exposure. The fearful are caught as often as the bold.'

Therefore the real question is: Is it *work worth doing* ... or not?

If it is, then to get there you'll need to get a move on. But do so knowing that not everything is going to go just as you'd like it. There will be hurdles.

It will require hustle. At times it will be hard going. Lonely even. There may be some people you grow apart from and others who'll criticise your efforts or let you down. You might even let yourself down — not intentionally, of course. But you may get distracted or do something to get in your own way. Maybe you'll focus on the wrong thing, miss an important detail or make the wrong call.

Such is life. The bigger your goals, the more challenges you're inviting into your life. This is not negative thinking; it's just basic math. Let's face it, if it were easy to live a big life and accomplish extraordinary things, more people would! An *extra*-ordinary life requires extra from you. Extra work, extra courage, extra commitment, extra trust in yourself.

IT IS WHO YOU MUST BECOME ON YOUR QUEST TOWARDS YOUR HIGHEST ASPIRATIONS THAT MAKES THEIR PURSUIT WORTHWHILE.

Poet Robert Browning once wrote that 'the aim, if reached or not, makes great the life'. It's why it makes far more sense to pursue what lights you up instead of pursuing happiness. Happiness is the bi-product of moving towards what inspires you.

Side note: If you are totally content sticking with the comfort of your life right now, knock yourself out. Just a word of warning though: your comfort zone can be a beautiful place, but nothing grows there. Accordingly, what is comfortable now won't stay comfortable forever. After all, if you're not growing, you're shrinking.

EMBRACE DISCOMFORT AS A PRE-REQUISITE FOR YOUR GROWTH.

That's because we need to grow in order to thrive. Like grapes on a vine, if we aren't growing, we shrivel up. So while a part of us may only want to do what's comfortable, if we go with that option we deprive ourselves of the very opportunities to evolve and grow our muscles. And when muscles aren't being used, they begin to atrophy, along with our confidence for anything new. It's why people who've not left their comfort zone since the moon landing don't age well, and feel increasingly anxious at any whiff of change.

Do not underestimate the toll of opting for a life of 'immaculate mediocrity', trading long-term fulfilment for short-term comfort. It might look good right now, but it won't feel good later on.

IF YOU AREN'T INTENTIONAL ABOUT CREATING A FUTURE YOU WANT, YOU RISK ENDING UP SOME PLACE YOU DON'T.

The most 'lit up' people I've had the good fortune to meet in my life are not those who wander along the 'default path' of life, taking what comes and waiting for opportunity to knock. Rather, they live from design, deliberately creating a future that lights them up and putting themselves in good luck's path. They pursue diverse paths — some are bohemian artists, others are teachers, others are running their own tech startups and others are working in not-for-profit social enterprises. Some make lots of money, others just enough to get by. Sometimes they achieve incredible things; other times, they hit walls and have to find new, more creative paths forward.

But what they all have in common is that what they do every day is meaningful to them and aligns with their deepest values and highest aspirations. And while they sometimes nail their goals, and sometimes don't, they don't linger and languish on the sidelines of life, filling their days wandering store aisles, scrolling social media feeds or sitting around critiquing those who have dared to risk the odd misstep and enter the arena. Rather they spend their best hours and years immersed in their own 'work worth doing', returning to the bench only for as long as it takes to recharge, reset and reconnect to the source of what inspired them to set out to begin with.

What excites you? What dream or idea lights you up, even if it also immediately triggers a tsunami of overwhelm, misgivings and self-doubts at the enormity of the journey ahead? Doubts have a way of doing that; of trailing your dreams like a shadow. The more daring your ambition, the longer the shadow. You can't make a shadow disappear, but, as I wrote in the last chapter, you have the power to keep it from downsizing your dreams. As Geneen Roth pointed out in *This Messy Magnificent Life*, 'fear isn't a monster, it's a feeling'. One you have the courage to overcome.

So back to my question:

What vision calls you into action, even if it exceeds your current capacity to bring it into reality?

If you're not really sure, don't stress. Sometimes you have to sit in the wilderness of 'not knowing' for a while and give your future possibilities space to slowly crystallise.

What matters right now is that you're willing to play with those possibilities — to simply sit in curious wonder about what your future *could* be; about who *you* could be. As comedian Lily Tomlin once said, 'I always wanted to be somebody … I should have been more specific.'

IT'S THE DIRECTION YOU'RE HEADED THAT COUNTS, NOT THE DESTINATION.

Sometimes it takes something extreme to give us the clarity of direction or reveal a higher purpose in our lives. When I was 28 and working in corporate marketing in Papua New Guinea I found myself in the midst of an armed robbery. One of the robbers thrust a sawn-off shotgun into my forehead before realising I was unable to access the cash payroll for our local staff. Once he did, I was told to get on the floor. Laying face down on the ground, I felt one of the men put his hand up my skirt and groped me. For several minutes my greatest fear was not that I'd be killed but that I'd be taken back to their village settlement and gang raped. This was not uncommon in PNG.

I was eighteen weeks pregnant at the time. Ten days later, at my nineteen-week scan, I was told that the baby I thought was alive and soon to begin a regular somersault routine in my belly had died. I wrote about this traumatic crucible experience in *Brave* (and the revised edition, *Train the Brave*), but share it again here because it became the catalyst for me to reset my career compass and enrol in a postgraduate psychology program. I had absolutely no idea where it would take me at the time. However, inspired by the writings of Wayne Dyer and M. Scott Peck, I just knew I needed to heed the deep calling I felt to empower people to live their lives with greater purpose and courage.

About a year later, seven months pregnant with my first child, Lachlan, I moved from PNG back to Melbourne, Australia, as Andrew took up a new role. It had been a pretty anxious twelve months as we'd had two more early miscarriages and then tiptoed anxiously through my pregnancy with Lachlan, so I was excited to be back closer to family and friends. We bought a cute little home, which we moved into when Lachlan was six weeks old. While he was a voracious feeder who kept me perpetually sleep deprived, I took to motherhood easily, probably drawing on all my years as the bottle-making big sister.

When Lachlan was about eight months old, Andrew's company wanted him to relocate again, this time interstate to Adelaide. I was none too thrilled about this, not just because I didn't know anyone in Adelaide but because I was also pregnant again. But move we did, and so I arrived in Adelaide seven months pregnant with Maddy. While I'd cried my way to the airport, once I landed I wiped away my 'woe is me' tears and set about trying to make some friends. I immersed myself in the local 'play groups' so that by the time Maddy arrived (just fifteen months after Lachlan) I had a social support network to lean on.

Six relatively sleep-deprived months later, the university where I'd started my psychology studies three years earlier contacted me. 'Would you like to resume?' I pondered it for a while: I had two children under two, had been pregnant or breastfeeding around the clock for a few years, and I was perpetually exhausted. Should I resume studies or not? And if so, when on earth would I fit it in? I hardly had a moment to myself each day, and when I did at night, my brain was mush. So I decided to do a guided meditation on a Wayne Dyer CD and by the end of it, I was clear about the right path of action: return to study. I still wasn't sure where my studies would take me, but it was affirming to be moving in a general direction, however glacially slow, that aligned with my growing passion to support others in finding their own direction!

At the time I had no childcare as I didn't feel comfortable spending money on extra help when I wasn't working. But the stars aligned via a 'babysitter available' ad on the noticeboard at the local library. Vicky, a semi-retiree, was looking for a little extra cash to supplement her pension. Perfect! So each Friday morning at 8 am Vicky would arrive, and while the kids were distracted with the Wiggles I'd sneak out to the local library to study. Many of my new mother friends thought I was a little odd (or totally crazy) to use my one child-free window each week to study. All I knew was that engaging a part of my brain four hours a week that was not used for the other 164 hours made me feel better about myself, providing some sense of identity and utility beyond that of being a mother (as noble a calling as motherhood is!)

Several times I deferred my studies in between having my four children and moving home multiple times, including relocating to the United States weeks after 9/11, again with Andrew's work. A few years into my stop-start studies, a guy I met at a dinner party recommended I check out this new thing called coaching. After confirming that this type of coaching did not require any hand-eye coordination (of which I'm in scant possession), upon completing my graduate psychology studies, I got certified as an executive life coach and set about building a 'coaching practice', as I called it back then. The idea of writing books, giving speeches, being the 'resident coach' on a national morning TV show, running retreats, interviewing global leaders ... none of these were part of that original vision. Not one. While what unfolded was largely organic, the common thread through all these adventures has always been to help people live braver lives.

If there is one overriding lesson from my own experience, it is not to wait until you have a vision that you could paint in fine brushstrokes before you start out. Nor a bullet-proof business plan. Or even a half-baked one.

Start moving towards whatever it is that tugs at your heart, or even just piques your curiosity right now. Your vision will evolve as you do.

Just promise me this:

That you won't sit still.

And if you happen to be in your twenties, this means you won't buy into the misguided idea that your twenties are for wasting.

No time is for wasting.

Resting, yes. Playing, exploring, trying things out: yes. Sitting under a tree contemplating your life, yes. But wasting — scrolling mindlessly on social media, celebrity gossip sites or partying/shopping/numbing/escaping yourself for hours/days/years on end — *never*.

And if you happen to be up to your ears with raising boundlessly beautiful but relentlessly exhausting little people, this means accepting that there is a season for everything, but it doesn't mean you can't still do something, however small or insignificant it might feel, that will be laying the groundwork for something bigger for your future.

IF YOU WAIT FOR PERFECT CONDITIONS, YOU'LL WASTE YOUR BEST YEARS IN A WAITING ROOM.

If you're in your forties or fifties or sixties or far beyond, refuse to let the number of years you've been alive be your excuse for not taking the actions you might wish you'd taken years ago; the actions that would add a whole new dimension to your life today. As my friend Rich Kaarlgard wrote in *Late Bloomers*, 'Blooming has no deadline. Our future story is written in pencil, not carved in stone. It can be changed. There is no fixed chronology to self-determination, no age limit for breakthroughs'.

Julia Child was 49 when she wrote her first cookbook.

Laura Ingalls Wilder didn't start writing until her forties, and didn't pen *Little House on the Prairie* until she was in her sixties.

Vera Wang was 39 before she started designing clothes.

Colonel Harland Sanders was in his sixties when he started Kentucky Fried Chicken.

Diana Nyad was 64 when, after four failed attempts spanning 36 years, she finally achieved her long-held ambition of swimming the infamous channel of shark-ridden waters from Cuba to Florida (without a shark cage).

Sure, it would have been great had you started five or fifteen years ago, but you didn't know then what you know now. And sure, some windows may have closed. That's what windows do. But there are still plenty of others waiting to be opened. And you likely could not have opened them if you hadn't had every single experience you've had up to this point. Because each and every experience you've had — particularly the tough ones that knocked you flat or left you feeling deflated, humiliated, humbled or heartbroken — were catalysts for you to learn and discover and grow into the person you are today.

I mean, just imagine who you'd be today if you'd gotten everything you'd ever wanted or if everything you'd ever touched had turned to gold with little effort. If you'd never felt the sting of rejection or the kick in the guts of failing at something, you wouldn't be half the person you are today.

So whatever your age, whatever your situation, whatever the setbacks you've faced or the heartaches you've nursed or the stories you've told yourself about who you are and what you can do (or what you *cannot* do), decide right now that you will not settle for a life (career, relationships, etc.) that doesn't light you up. More so, that you will set your sights on whatever vision — however humble or scarily huge — that does light you up. Research shows that while we lose some abilities as we grow older, the benefits of those we gain far exceed any that are lost. So rather than ask, 'What can I accomplish despite my struggles?', ask yourself, 'What can I accomplish *because* of them?'

START WITH WHAT YOU HAVE, NOT WHAT YOU WANT. LIFE REWARDS ACTION.

Vision = Power

A vision acts like a compass to help you discern how you will spend your time, who you will spend it with, the skills you will gain and the strengths you will develop.

Just because someone once told you that you didn't have what it takes, it doesn't mean you don't.

And just because there are plenty of other people who seem to have more talent and skill and stuff going for them than you, it doesn't mean you don't have everything you need at this very precise moment of your one and only precious life to get started.

Remember Brenda? She'd never have taken the first step in launching her own line of active wear had she got stuck comparing her knowledge and skills and résumé with the likes of Lorna Jane or Lululemon's founders.

Start where you are. With what you have. And trust that if the dream has somehow lodged its way in your heart and mind then it's there for a reason.

ALLOW YOURSELF TO RATE AS 'NEEDS IMPROVEMENT' STARTING OUT

I'd never have attempted my first book, *Find Your Courage*, much less this one, if I'd gone down the rabbit hole of comparing my literary prowess with that of Elizabeth Gilbert, or my wisdom with that of Maya Angelou. So beware of comparing where you are now with someone who's been in the game a long time, or comparing your current skill level with someone who's been practising your craft for years. Give yourself permission, as Anne Lamott wrote in *Bird by Bird*, to do a 'shitty first draft'. Because only when you've created a really lousy first draft can you get to create a slightly-less-lousy second draft. And from there, eventually, move on to a half reasonable one.

You've got to start somewhere.

Right here, right now, is as good a place as any.

Daniel Gilbert, a research psychologist at Harvard, spent years studying happiness. One of his key findings is that when people take a risk in their lives — changing jobs, starting a business, moving, returning to study, getting hitched — even when the gamble doesn't pay off as they'd hoped (e.g. that Tinder date did not turn into the love of their life, or look remotely like their profile picture), they are almost always glad they took it.

Gilbert's research found that while nine out of ten people *think* they will regret foolish action more than foolish inaction, just the opposite is true. As he wrote in *Stumbling on Happiness*, 'In the long run, people of every age and in every walk of life seem to regret *not* having done things much more than they regret things they *did*.' Turns out, our psychological immune system can rationalise an excess of courage more easily than an excess of cowardice.

So indulge me for a moment with a little exercise.

CONSULT WITH YOUR FUTURE SELF

Every possibility begins with the courage to imagine. So wherever you are right now, take a deep breath, read through these instructions and then close your eyes and use your imagination to answer them. The size of your life will unfold in direct proportion to the size of your vision.

Imagine yourself in the twilight years of your life, many years from now. What life would you love to be looking back on? What would the older, wiser and more lived version of your true self be encouraging you to do if it could whisper into your ear right now, as you read these words?

Where might your more evolved future self be encouraging you to raise your sights? What dream would it urge you to pursue? What talent or passion would it be encouraging you to nurture? What change would it be urging you to make? What attachment or story or grudge would it want you to let go of?

Connect to that vision. Listen to the urgings of the highest self you can one day become.

Now wind the clock to five years from now. How old will you be? Once again, imagine yourself living out your ultimate life. You may still be in action towards long-term aspirations, but you feel 'on purpose' and connected to your deepest truth and supported by those you've surrounded yourself with. Imagine what you'd be doing and feeling as your present reality.

Where would you be? What activities would fill your days? Who would be around you? How would you be growing, and giving, and experiencing your life each day? Step into that future in your mind's eye and 'feel it in your bones'. Connect with the heart space of your future self. Feel the emotions that would dominate your days. Anchor them into your heart.

We are all born unique, with our own lessons to learn, our own gifts to share, our own sacred contract to fulfil and hero's journey to complete. So if there is some vision, aspiration or idea that keeps appearing in your mind or tugging at your heartstrings, then it does so for a reason.

Trust your vision, then trust yourself to figure it out each step of the way as you move towards it. Every great endeavour begins with a daring first step.

If you watched the movie *Sliding Doors* with Gwyneth Paltrow, you'll appreciate the idea that there are moments that can forever change the course of our lives. In this case, in one scenario, Helen (Paltrow) is fired from her job and rushes to catch the train home, only to discover her boyfriend in bed with another woman. In the second, she misses the train and arrives home after the woman has left. In the first, she dumps her boyfriend, finds a new man and gets on with a better life (and haircut). In the second, she gradually grows suspicious of his infidelity and becomes increasingly miserable.

In this movie, fate alone determines which life she lives. But consider that right now you have the opportunity to make a decision that could forever change the trajectory of your life. If you stick with the familiar and comfortable safety of where you are now, you might be leaving on the table a whole unlived life that could be infinitely more rewarding than your current default existence. Sure, many life-changing factors are outside your control. Yes, trains can arrive late and tragedy can strike from nowhere. Yet you can decide to take new actions, and embrace any psychological discomfort as the prerequisite for your growth and success that it is. And then, tomorrow, you can make that choice again, clear in knowing that while you risk short-term vulnerability, you spare yourself the far greater risk of missing out on a whole other life.

People often ask 'What would you do if you weren't afraid to fail?' A far better question is to ask:

What is so important to you that, even if you fell short, you would never regret having tried?

Embrace ambition. Dial up your daring. Set your sights on a vision that compels you to throw off the bowlines and set sail towards whatever port most lights you up. Then, and only then, can you ever grow into your full potential.

Trust that if you have a vision that lights you up, it's because it's within you to bring it to reality. Sure, some doors you may have hoped would open will fail to do so. So be it. In the end it matters far less what you achieve than who you become in the process of daring to pursue whatever sets your heart on fire. 'But what if I fail?' you ask. But oh, what if you fly? As Eric Hanson wrote, 'There is freedom waiting for you on the breezes of the sky'.

Take the leap; your wings are stronger than you know.

Work worth doing is waiting.

the
growing

'A moment of self-compassion can change your entire day. A string of such moments can change your life.'

Christopher Germer

4

Embrace Your Fallibility
Get off your own back and forgive your failings!

I arrived at my hotel in Nashville in the early afternoon. The following morning I was to be the opening keynote speaker at a large conference hosted by a Silicon Valley tech company. I had a pile of work to do (like writing this book), and so I ordered a late lunch via room service. After eating my salad, I placed the tray outside my door and kept the fruit cup for later. After a few hours, I decided to take a short nap and took off my jeans before lying down. When I got up, I decided to eat the fruit. Of course, I could have eaten it with my fingers but I thought I'd just check if my lunch tray was still outside the door so I could grab the fork I'd left on it. I popped my head out and sure enough, it was. Bending over to grab the fork, I kept my foot wedged in the door behind me, just as I'd done when I put the tray out. But alas, it mustn't have been wedged quite far enough back because *bam*, the door locked shut behind me.

So there I was, stranded in the hallway, on the top executive floor of the hotel, in just a t-shirt and knickers. No pants. No room key. And no place to hide!

If that wasn't bad enough, the hotel was almost entirely booked out by those attending my conference. So as I stood there, trying to process what I had just done, I realised that the people exiting the elevator around the corner and walking past me, mostly middle-aged men in blazers, wearing lanyards from the pre-conference workshops that day, were almost certainly going to be among the audience in my opening plenary session the following morning.

I was mortified. If I could have dug a hole in the hotel floor, I'd have buried myself in it.

There was not a cupboard in sight and, being on the 21st floor, I didn't dare make a dash for the elevator to make my way down to the crowded lobby below. At that moment another man walked past me and smiled. I half-smiled back. Had he noticed I had no pants on? He had taken a few steps past me when I decided I needed his help.

'Ummm ... excuse me ...' he turned around to see who I was talking to. 'I am having a very embarrassing moment,' I said, accentuating *very*. 'You see, I've just locked myself out of my room and I'm wondering if you could get someone to let me in.'

'You don't have a room key?' he asked, clearly clarifying if he'd misheard me.

'Ah, no, I don't. And I don't have any pants on either.'

He briefly glanced down and, seeing this was indeed a fact, looked back up at my blushing face and nodded awkwardly in agreement.

'I'll see what I can do,' he said, then walked off around the corner towards the elevators, I assumed to seek help for this semiclad damsel in distress.

I spied a housekeeping cart a few doors down the hallway and looked through a few peepholes to see if I could spot anyone cleaning a room. But I couldn't, and I didn't dare knock on a door lest it was a guest. Or worse, some VIP who'd been invited to the VIP book signing reception I was doing after my presentation the next morning.

At this point the man who I had assumed had caught the elevator to get help walked back past me. As he did, he asked again, 'So you don't have a room key?'

'No, I definitely don't,' I confirmed, wondering why he'd assume I'd have been standing there, in just a t-shirt and knickers, if I did. He continued down the hallway.

Unsure what to do, I crouched down by my food tray in a futile attempt to make myself as inconspicuous as possible as other executive-looking men walked past me to their rooms. I probably looked like a homeless person rummaging through left-over scraps, but by this point keeping my face from full view was my chief concern.

I looked up to see the man I'd spoken to walking back towards me. He held a robe outstretched in his hands. 'You might want to put this on while you wait. Someone from security is coming.'

Somehow I had the presence of mind to ask him his name.

'George' he replied, and, looking rather uncomfortable about the whole thing, he once again disappeared around the corner towards the elevators.

When I finally got let back into my room (a five-minute wait that felt like five hours), I desperately needed to unload my embarrassment on someone. It was too early to call Andrew in Singapore, so I tried to call my assistant, Angela. When she didn't answer I filmed a short video on my phone and sent it to her and Andrew. She replied a few minutes later, 'OMG, I am crying. You've *got* to post this on Insta.' And so, I swallowed my pride, embraced my vulnerability and uploaded it. Two and half minutes of me sharing how mortified I was and pondering if I should share the story the following morning during my keynote. Within minutes people started responding with a lot of red-faced laughing emojis and an overwhelming 'Yes! George is a hero.'

So as I stepped on stage the following morning, I took a deep breath and shared my embarrassing ordeal. At the end of my story, I held up the robe, which I'd brought down and left side stage, and said, 'If anyone out there called George is missing a robe, I'd like to give you the Golden Robe Award for saving me yesterday.'

I think it's fair to say, the audience laughed both with me and *at* me. My decision to throw myself under the vulnerability bus had been validated.

After my talk I headed to the VIP reception for their key clients where I was asked to autograph copies of my book *Stop Playing Safe*. Well, lo and behold, who should walk up to me, reclaimed robe in hand, but George.

Oh boy did I laugh. 'You saved me!' I said. At which point he confided that he'd thought I was a country singer in Nashville to perform and assumed he'd never see me again. So you can imagine his surprise when the pant-less woman he'd encountered in the hallway the day before walked up onto the stage to deliver the opening keynote address at his convention.

Clearly there are a few morals to this story.

One: Never leave your room without your room key, but definitely don't do it without pants on! It's extremely embarrassing.

Two: Lighten up on yourself. If you think you're gonna look back one day and laugh, don't wait.

Three: Embrace your humanity and share your fallen moments with others. It not only makes you more real and relatable, but it makes others feel better about their own mishaps (even if less embarrassing than yours).

And four: If you are going to leave your hotel room without either a key or being fully dressed, at least wear your finest underwear.

Of course, I'm hoping that you will never find yourself in the situation I did. However, I know I'm not the only who's ever done something they soon came to regret (albeit likely less embarassing).

In fact I'm guessing there's been a few times you've beaten up on yourself for not having it all together.

You're such an idiot.

What were you thinking?

Seriously? Everyone else has this figured out.

When will you ever learn and get your act together?!

Let's face it: we can be far harder on ourselves than anyone else ever can. As Arianna Huffington says, 'Even our worst enemies don't talk about us the way we talk to ourselves,' describing her inner critic as the obnoxious roommate in her head. It's why trusting that 'you've got this' — particularly in those moments when you've fallen short of the idealised image of who you'd like to be — requires being really intentional about how you speak to yourself, lest the voice of your inner critic/obnoxious roommate drown out any other.

Many people have a well-ingrained habit of psychological self-battery. Perhaps you're one of them. If so, I reckon it's about time you considered how else you could respond when your actions fall short of the high bar you set for yourself.

LIGHTEN UP AND STOP TAKING YOURSELF SO SERIOUSLY. IF THERE'S ANY CHANCE YOU'LL ONE DAY LOOK BACK AND LAUGH, DON'T WAIT.

Sure, my 'special moment' in Nashville was embarrassing, but it was not the end of the world. Nor did the sky fall in the time I interviewed Bill Marriott on stage at a town hall meeting at Marriott's headquarters with a long streak of blood down my legs from a rushed shaving mishap that morning. Nor did it kill me when I did a live TV interview without realising my dress had hitched up showing far (as in *far far*) more thigh than was seemly. Nor did my career end when I made a typo in an article published on a high-profile online media platform, referring to the 'pubic' failure of a world leader who'd kindly offered their thoughts for my column. (And was promptly contacted by someone in this shall-not-be-named leader's office to promptly rectify it after their boss had spotted my proof-reading oversight.) I could go on, but you get my point (besides not relying on spell check).

We all mess up. In small ways, in big ways, in bloody ways, in embarrassing ways. Sometimes we make highly 'pubic' failures that everyone can see — or read about — in the gossip columns.

But here's the deal: if you're showing up fully for life, putting yourself 'out there' (though not necessarily in hotel hallways), then missteps are bound to happen. Yet as Kathy Calvin, President of the United Nations Foundation, shared with me in an interview (devoid of wardrobe failures), 'The mistakes you make matter far less than what you do immediately after them.'

You can beat up on yourself. Plunge yourself into a shame spiral. Hide away in a cave. Drown your sorrows. Blame them on someone else (which can, let's face it, be quite satisfying in the moment).

Or 'all of the above'.

My experience? None of these will land you in a better place. More likely, a worse one.

What's more effective is embracing your full humanity and being a little gentler on yourself, particularly when you want to bang your head (or someone else's) against a wall. And if you can possibly find a way to laugh at your situation, then go right ahead. My personal experience is that a hearty dose of humour coupled with 100 per cent responsibility (resisting the temptation to blame the nearest scapegoat!) can be a highly effective way of dealing with even the worst screw-ups. In fact, a study by Nicholas Kuiper and Rod Martin from the University of Western Ontario found that people with high levels of humour who laughed more often not only had more 'positive affect' (i.e. they felt more positive emotions) in good situations, but they coped better in difficult situations and emerged from them with stronger self-esteem. The takeaway: laughter has a medicinal effect that transcends your health. It's like therapy, but cheaper, and works best when directed at yourself.

THE WORLD'S FULL OF CRITICS PULLING OTHERS
DOWN TO PROP THEMSELVES UP. IT'S JUST
ONE MORE REASON TO BE YOUR OWN BEST
CHEERLEADER, NOT YOUR HARSHEST CRITIC.

Of course, I am a work in progress, but over the years I've gradually got better at catching my inner critic as it pipes up. Rather than descending into full-blown self-flagellation in the wake of a setback, disappointment or mistake, I think of what a good friend or compassionate figure I admire would say to me in that moment. The person I think of depends on the situation. Sometimes it's actually not a person but a higher source, as I share in chapter 5. So when time permits, I'll get out my journal (I'm a life-long journal devotee) and write down what someone who really loves me, or a higher loving power, would want me to know in that moment. The responses often go something like this.

Dear Margie ...

Go easy on yourself. You've got a lot on your plate.

So it didn't go as you wanted. Such is life. Find the lesson and move on, a little wiser.

You're in the arena, and sometimes it's hard. But hard isn't always bad. Hard is how you grow.

What others say or do never defines your worth. You do.

If it were easy to pursue big dreams, everyone would be doing it.

You'll figure this out ... one step, one day at a time.

Keep faith and press on.

You've got this!

So next time you feel tempted to use your fallen moments as a cudgel to beat up on yourself, try talking to yourself as the kindest or wisest or funniest person you admire might do in your predicament. That is, with compassion, patience, empathy, warmth and, when required, a hearty dose of humour.

WE ALL WRESTLE WITH OUR OWN HARDSHIPS AND HEARTACHES, INSECURITIES AND STRUGGLES. JUST BECAUSE YOU CAN'T SEE OTHERS' INNER BATTLES DOESN'T MEAN THEY'RE NOT WAGING THEM.

When I share with people what I'm wrestling with and they respond by sharing what's keeping them up at night, it often makes me feel a little better about my own problems, even if they're dealing with something completely different.

I don't share my challenges with people in the twisted hope that theirs will be worse. Rather, I share them knowing that we're all wrestling with our own 'stuff', engaged in our own inner struggles, and that I'm not the only one wrangling with life, yet to figure out how to navigate a future I hadn't reckoned on. (That said, I don't know anyone in my precise predicament, so if you ever come across someone raising four kids and juggling dual careers across multiple continents, send them my way. I've got a bottle chilling.)

There were so many times when my kids were young that I felt like I was struggling more than the other mothers around me. My kids seemed to fight more, and louder, and I seemed to drop more balls than most. (I suspect having four kids in five years had something to do with this.) Yet my friendships with other mothers who openly shared and laughed about their own 'motherhood fails' helped keep me sane. There was something comforting about knowing I wasn't the only one to lose my temper at an impetuous three-year-old or forget to pick up a child from an after-school activity. Though I think I'm the only one who ever had their kids pick bouquets of 'wildflowers' (a.k.a. weeds) on the nature strip outside their school when I pulled up at the morning 'drop off' to realise it was teacher appreciation day. As other children were filing into school holding beautiful bouquets, Belgian chocolates and handcrafted cards, I said to my kids, what matters most is that you've picked these weeds flowers with love. Back then they still believed everything I said so it was all good.

Since this isn't a parenting book, I will spare you my full laundry list of parenting failures (that would be a book in itself!). However, I'm happy to report that despite my deficiencies as a mother my kids are all growing into grounded, resilient and good-humoured young adults. (Perhaps from all the practice they got picking weeds and my many dropped balls?)

The truth is that we're all in this 'human-becoming' game together. And while you may sometimes feel like you're alone with your problems, I can assure you that everyone around you is struggling in their own way with something. So whatever you're dealing with right now, and whatever 'missed-takes' you've made over the years (which is what a mistake actually is), embrace all of it as part and parcel of the universal human experience of life.

Recognising your connection to others, embracing your humanity and accepting your struggles as an intrinsic part of being human — rather than as proof of your inadequacy — helps you carry your load better and keeps you from getting caught up dwelling on your shortcomings. Numerous studies by Kristin Neff, a researcher in self-compassion, have found that recognising our common humanity allows us to be more understanding and less judgemental about our inadequacies and not let them define us.

BE VELCRO FOR THE GOOD, NOT FOR THE BAD. WHAT YOU PLACE YOUR ATTENTION UPON SHAPES HOW YOU EXPERIENCE YOUR LIFE.

Many years ago when I was first starting to speak publicly (initially as a means to get coaching clients, since I'd only moved to the US two years earlier), I gave a free 'brown bag' talk at the Dallas headquarters of a large airline. It was about how to have 'courageous conversations' at work, and during my talk I impersonated someone saying, 'Oh my God, I just hate confrontation.' The following day, my point of contact at the company who'd helped to organise the session emailed to say feedback had been overwhelmingly positive except for one complaint.

A complaint?!*?!

I recall feeling like I'd been kicked in the gut. Someone had complained ... about *me*? I racked my mind trying to think what on earth I'd done to warrant it. Upon coming up empty, I rang her up to find out. 'Apparently, you blasphemed,' she said, a little coyly.

I did?

'I don't recall you doing so, but apparently you used the Lord's name in vain. But don't worry about it,' she assured me. 'Everyone else thought you were terrific.'

But it was too late. My self-flagellation had begun. That one bit of negative feedback from some very pious person had totally overshadowed all the praise.

You've probably had a similar experience yourself. Maybe in a performance review where 99 per cent of the feedback was great but you focused on the 1 per cent that wasn't. Which just goes to show we are all wired with a negativity bias. When something happens that makes us feel bad, we hold on to that negative emotion, letting it stick to us like velcro. And when something great happens, we often don't allow ourselves to let it really sink in, so it rolls right off us as though we're coated in Teflon. Which is why we have to be extra diligent not to let the bad stuff stick and to let the good stuff sink in.

What you focus on amplifies in your headspace. So stop focusing on what's missing or wrong, and start focusing on what's present and right.

We have about 60 000 thoughts a day. Many of which tend to revolve around what we *don't* want, *don't* have or *can't* do. This presents a problem! You see, whatever you focus your attention on is magnified and tends to attract more of the same into your life. If you focus on how sick you feel, you'll feel even sicker and catch every virus that enters your orbit. If you focus on how stressful life is, you'll feel even more stressed and land yourself in more situations that trigger stress. And if you always focus on what's wrong and what's missing and who's to blame, you'll feel constantly 'less than' and frustrated ... with yourself or someone else.

It's why cultivating mindfulness can be so incredibly transformative. At the heart of mindfulness is paying attention to what you are paying attention to; to notice your thoughts and hold them with what the Zen masters call 'warm and loving regard'.

One tool for doing this is through 'mirror meditation' — a technique based on the neuroscience of mirroring and psychological research on empathy, self-compassion and emotional resilience. Pioneered by my friend Tara Well, a psychologist at Barnard College of Columbia University, it involves simply looking at your reflection in a mirror and paying attention to your thoughts as they come up. As you observe your own facial expressions, the mirror brings to light how self-critical you can be (of your appearance and other aspects of yourself), giving you the opportunity to replace your judgement with kindness and acceptance. This practice not only fosters greater self-awareness and self-compassion, but it helps you be more empathetic with others, growing your capacity for more authentic relationships.

I have spent a significant part of my life reinforcing the mental habit of attending more to my flaws, faults and failings than to my gifts, strengths and accomplishments. I know I'm not alone in this. But if you relate at all, then I've got good news. You can change this! You see, our brains have an innate plasticity, which means that no matter how good you've been at focusing on the bad, you can retrain your brain the other way.

In recent years I've become much better at catching myself when my innate negativity bias has me being overly hard on myself, judging my thoughts and feelings as wrong or weak. The same is possible for you. Your brain is not a machine, hardwired like a computer. In fact, it's very pliable and, most importantly, it stays that way throughout our lives. Norman Doidge, a psychiatrist and researcher who wrote a brilliant book called *The Brain that Changes Itself,* said that the neuroplasticity of our brains 'not only gives hope to those with mental limitations but expands our understanding of the healthy brain and the resilience of human nature'.

> MENTAL HABITS AREN'T PERMANENTLY HARDWIRED.
> NO MATTER HOW SET YOUR WAYS, YOU CAN
> REWIRE YOUR THINKING TO LIFT YOU UP,
> NOT PULL YOU DOWN.

Neuropsychologist Donald Hebb first came up with the phrase 'Neurons that fire together, wire together' to describe how pathways in the brain are formed and reinforced through repetition. At the risk of oversimplifying a highly complex neural activity, our brain cells communicate with one another via synaptic transmission known as 'neuronal firing'. That is, one brain cell releases a chemical (neurotransmitter) that the next brain cell absorbs. So the more frequently brain cells communicate, the stronger their connection and the faster messages will travel along that same pathway in the future. It's why anyone who is masterful at a skill—from hitting a golf ball to playing violin to driving a car—will eventually go into autopilot. If you've ever driven to work and not remembered what you did to get there, you've experienced being in autopilot mode.

These same brain pathways process how you react to your environment, to the people around you and, yes, to yourself. More often than not people develop highly entrenched negative thought patterns that become very 'wired and fired' into our psyche. This doesn't mean it's impossible to change them, but it does mean it's going to take *lots* of practice.

A well-worn habit of beating up on yourself can play in a loop until you do something to consciously stop it. Different therapeutic approaches have been developed to stop the negative repetitive thought processes that can eventually lead to depression, anxiety, panic and obsessive compulsive behaviour. For instance, psychodynamic therapy 'processes' the thoughts in a way that the useful parts are kept, and the harmful parts are discarded.

The good news is that we are not powerless to short-circuit negative loops and establish positive ones that improve our emotional state. By paying attention to what you're saying to yourself when your inner critic fires up, and then replacing the malevolent voice with a benevolent one, you can, over time, retrain your brain. In short, if you keep practising being nicer to yourself when you want to berate yourself, over time, being kinder to yourself will become your default. I know this works because I've experienced it! As Martin Seligman wrote in *Learned Optimism*, 'Habits of thinking need not be forever.' No matter what your age, you can always learn new ones. Put another way, the idea that you 'can't teach an old dog new tricks' is simply untrue.

SHOW A LITTLE MERCY FOR YOURSELF OR YOU'LL ALWAYS BE AN EXILE IN YOUR OWN LIFE.

By embracing your own humanity — accepting yourself for all that you are *and* for all that you aren't — you can savour more moments of gratitude, joy and connection over the course of an ordinary day and spare yourself feelings of isolation, inadequacy and unworthiness.

While this actually is brain science, it's far from an earth-shattering headline. It's just that many of us get stuck in a fixed mindset, buying into the mistaken belief that we cannot change. It's why we need reminding again and again and again.

You're not perfect. You never will be. But most of all, you're not supposed to be!

And if, by some bizarre stroke of Mother Nature, you had been born 'perfect' (though how on earth anyone would measure that I'm not sure), you would not be remotely near as real or relatable or awesome as you are. And quite frankly, if your life were some idealised version of 'perfect' (think of the Stepford wives), then I can tell you right now that it would be mind-numbingly boring.

As my beautiful friend and fellow coach/author/speaker/figure-it-out-as-we-go-alongerer Michelle McQuaid shared on my Live Brave podcast, it's our rough edges that give others something to hold on to.

Just think about the people in your life who you admire the most — the ones you cherish like gold (as I do Michelle). You'll notice something they all share in common. Not one of them is perfect. Not even close to perfect. Some may even get on your goat at times. Yet despite their faults and failings, you love them anyway (well, most of the time). And you know what? Despite your faults and failings, they love you too (most of the time).

Which is entirely my point — you don't have to be infallible to be fabulous; you don't have to be up for a Nobel Peace Prize to be prized, and you don't have to have a spotless track record to be worthy of love, affection or admiration. We are all innately flawed and fallible. Only when we embrace the full spectrum of our humanity can we transcend our shadows and step fully into our own light.

And the best part? By giving yourself permission to not have it *all* together, *all* the time, you liberate yourself to try things you might otherwise not attempt, to express yourself more authentically, to celebrate your wins more joyously, to appreciate your gifts more fully and to trust in yourself more deeply. Pretty cool, huh?

Of the many burdens we foist onto ourselves, perfectionism is among the heaviest. So, if you are exhausted from years of continually beating up on yourself, consider how it would serve you — today and in the years of your life stretching out ahead — if you cut yourself a little slack and gave yourself permission to be a little bit less perfect and a little bit more human.

WHAT YOU APPRECIATE APPRECIATES

Where traditional psychology is focused on dysfunction, the field of positive psychology distinguishes itself by focusing on what *is* working and draws out our best. Focusing on the positive aspects of our shared human experience, it helps us (and the teams and communities we're part of) to draw on our strengths to flourish and enjoy a deeper sense of meaning and wellbeing amid life's stream of pressures and uncertainty.

To that end, making it a daily habit to regularly reflect on what you did well, to celebrate your small wins and to appreciate your ongoing growth as a 'human becoming' helps to set you up to thrive — when life is going your way and, just as importantly, when it isn't.

Taking time to answer these five questions at the end of your day will help to reinforce your self-belief, encourage your growth and keep your attention on that which most serves you, not stifles you.

Five to Thrive

1. *What did I do well today?* No matter how badly you think you did, there will always be some positive action you took that deserves to be acknowledged.

2. *What am I grateful for?* Gratitude is one of life's most medicinal emotions. The more you practise it, the more you expand your capacity for joy and ability to feel truly wealthy regardless of your bank balance. List three things you're grateful for.

3. *What can I appreciate about myself?* A few moments of focused self-appreciation each day have a cumulative effect over time, helping you internalise that you truly are more worthy, capable, competent and all-round fabulous than you've been telling yourself. Write down three praise-worthy attributes.

4. *What did others appreciate about me today?* Spoken and unspoken. Consider the positive impact that you make on those around you. If you ever receive encouraging emails or notes, create a special place for them.

5. *What learning from today will I apply tomorrow?* Masters of life are also its best pupils. Every day holds lessons you can put into practice in the one ahead. Those you miss will require repeating. So write down the most important lesson(s) from today you can apply for the benefit of tomorrow.

Commit to writing your answers to these questions every day for a week. If it helps, even if just a little, stick with it until it's part of your daily routine (like brushing your teeth!).

ONLY WHEN YOU EMBRACE THE FULL SPECTRUM OF YOUR HUMANITY CAN YOU TRANSCEND ITS SHADOWS AND STEP FULLY INTO YOUR OWN LIGHT.

Oprah defines forgiveness as never again holding the past against someone. Likewise, self-forgiveness is about never again using *your past* against *yourself.*

There are many moments in everyone's life where we act in ways that are not aligned with our highest values. When we fail to think about how our actions will hurt others. When we give way to the temptation to lift ourselves up by putting others down. When we get stuck in jealousy, vindictiveness, pride, petulance.

I've done it. I'm guessing you've done it too.

I don't have to think too hard to recall flippant comments I've made that have caused offence. Or when I've been too quick to judge someone without taking the time to know them. Or when I've lacked the guts to deal with an awkward issue only to pay a steep price down the track. Or when I've totally lost it at my kids for acting like, well, kids. I could go on, but you get the gist. None of us are immune from the temptation to take the easier path, and every single one of us has, at one time or another, allowed short-term ego gratification to compromise our decisions.

The pull of pride, greed, jealousy, lust and fear can be strong. Very strong. Unless we regularly connect with the highest part of ourselves — that part that yearns to be generous and kind and brave and truthful — the pull of our small self can win out.

Perhaps you feel that your mistakes are far more grievous than losing patience with your kids or backing your car into a pylon (yep, did that too). Perhaps you are so filled with shame for what you did that you can't imagine how you could ever come to terms with your wrongs. Maybe people were hurt. Careers ruined. Fortunes lost. Hearts broken.

Denying hard truths serves no-one. However, we do not have to spend our lives living in shame for actions we cannot undo and wrongs we cannot unwind. But here's the deal: withholding forgiveness from yourself and choosing to suffer in shame and self-recrimination doesn't only hurt you, it hurts everyone you love. Or might ever love. That's because shame corrodes our sense of worthiness and keeps us from loving ourselves, much less trusting ourselves.

THE BEST SELF-HELP
BEGINS WITH SELF-COMPASSION.

Before I go on, let me just distinguish shame from guilt, as they are often confused. Where guilt says 'I did something bad', shame says 'I am bad'. It's why shame is so toxic, because it deprives you of the ability to learn the lessons your missteps hold (valuable lessons you could never have learnt otherwise) and to use your hard-won wisdom to be a greater gift for others. Shaming yourself for an action you cannot undo prevents you from taking action to make things more right. As Tara Brach wrote in *Radical Acceptance*, 'When we learn to face and feel the fear and shame we habitually avoid, we begin to awaken from trance.'

Of course, forgiving yourself doesn't mean others will forgive you for what you did. But that is their 'heart work' to do, not yours. So whether or not someone chooses to forgive you should never dictate whether you'll extend it to yourself. And, while it should go without saying, forgiving yourself for screwing up doesn't give you a free ride to be a jerk or justify actions that pull others down. It just gets you off the hook from wasting your precious energy tearing *yourself* down.

THE WORLD HAS NEVER SOUGHT YOUR INFALLIBILITY, IT SEEKS ONLY YOUR COURAGE.

At the heart of self-forgiveness is doing your own 'heart work': confronting with brutal self-honesty the deeper forces at play that led you to act as you did in the first place. And then 'cleaning up' your mess as best you can and recommitting yourself to do better next time. And, when you mess up again (as you will), to repeating this cycle.

(Please note: you will repeat the cycle many times.)

Now, if this all sounds like an easy way out, think again. Research shows that people who are better at extending compassion inward on themselves have higher levels of wellbeing and are more motivated, more resilient and more productive than people who aren't. In fact, Kristin Neff's research now shows that self-compassion is a stronger determinant for performance than self-esteem!

In short, forgiving yourself when you falter or fail isn't just the nice thing to do, it's the smart thing to do! So if you've been soaking in a guilt bath, it's time to get out of it and wrap yourself in a towel of mercy. To help you do this, I encourage you to reflect on these questions (they make a powerful journal exercise!):

Where am I withholding forgiving from myself?

How will holding on to guilt and shame continue to cost me and those I love?

What lessons have I learnt that I can use to be a better person and a greater gift to others?

So if you feel like you're not measuring up and have grown jaded by the endless advice on how to #liveyourbestlife, my best advice to you (and yes, no irony lost) is to cut yourself some slack and give yourself permission to be innately worthy and wholly imperfect ... at the same time! After all, the best self help always begins with self-compassion.

WHEN YOU MAKE PEACE WITH YOUR PAST AND
THROW OUT THE CASE YOU'VE MADE AGAINST
YOURSELF, YOU UNLEASH YOUR POTENTIAL
FOR GREATER THINGS.

I've had more than my usual share of 'uncomposed' moments in recent years, as best-laid plans have derailed and I've had to pick myself up from disappointments I'd not seen coming. Yet, as challenging as some moments have been, I've come to appreciate that our greatest growth and deepest fulfilment don't flow from the parts of us that are flawless or the times when life is sailing smoothly along. Rather, they flow from the parts of us we've been wrestling with our entire lives; those vulnerable corners of our being that dial up a notch or ten when plans go awry and life presses in (like when moving country with toddlers or teens ... something I've now managed to live through several times).

Those moments when I've felt anything but graceful, composed and put together have not only introduced me to new dimensions of courage, but they've taught me a great deal about self-compassion. In particular, that embracing our rawest moments is what makes us real, breaks us open and creates an opening to forge a more authentic connection to the truth in ourselves and in others.

Jack Kornfield says that, 'Compassion that doesn't include yourself is incomplete.' By ditching the idealistic yardstick we measure ourselves against, we liberate ourselves from the perpetual need to impress or prove or please (all of which can grow wearisome for all parties!). In doing so, we access a deeper dimension to our living, allowing more moments of genuine joy, gratitude, fulfilment and friendship to flow into our lives.

Just imagine the possibilities that could open up for you — in your relationships, career or creative expression — if you decided right now (and as often as you can manage it) to ground yourself in your innate 'enoughness', knowing that you don't have to be more or less of anything in order to be 'enough': to be worthy enough, ready enough, good enough.

But perhaps one of the most special things about getting off your own back and stepping out into the world as the one-of-a-kind fabulous 'n' fallible person that you are is that you give others permission to do the same. What greater gift is there?

(Besides handing someone a robe in their moment of need!)

'Run my dear
from anything that
would not strengthen
your precious
budding
wings.'

Hafez

5
Strengthen Your Wings
Expand your capacity to soar

The first time I ever saw someone jogging, my six-year-old brain wondered what on earth they were doing. We were driving along the single-lane country road between my parents' farm and my one-room school and there she was, doing the strangest of things: just running along on the gravel beside the road. Not chasing anything. Not running away from anything. She was wearing turquoise shorts and a bright terry-towelling headband, Olivia Newton-John style. I marvelled at the idea that someone would just go running for the sake of it (as distinct from trying to win the 100-metre egg and spoon race or get the heck out of the bull paddock after mistakenly wandering into it to pick wild mushrooms as I once did.)

I was soon to learn that her name was Mrs Oberg. Mrs Oberg was American, which was itself extremely novel and rather exotic in our rural area. My own mother was also technically an American, which always made her a little more exotic than other kids' mothers (at least to me). However, having set sail to Australia at age seven, Mum had long ago lost any traces of her accent, so, as my friends argued, she didn't really count. But Mrs Oberg, she had an accent. And she *looked* American. (It was the neon headband.) And she jogged … for fitness … along a quiet country road, every morning, in her turquoise shorts (or sometimes bright crimson ones).

It was many years later before I came to appreciate the benefits of jogging. And I was well in my thirties before I ever discovered, to my astonishment, that I was actually capable of jogging more than the length of the (not very big!) horse paddock myself, having bought into a story from my childhood that I was, as Dad used to call me, a 'bumblefoot' and somehow incapable of any athletic pursuit requiring anything beyond baseline coordination.

But I am not here to espouse the benefits of jogging, many as they are. Like hot yoga, pole dancing and Zumba, jogging is not everyone's cup of tea.

The only activity I'm promoting in this chapter is any activity that will expand your capacity to thrive, emboldening you to pursue what lights you up and bounce back faster when life pulls you down. That is, to do more of what fuels your courage to venture out onto that far limb and, drawing on the imagery of Victor Hugo, should the bough bend beneath you, to keep singing and not stress out, because your trust is in your wings and not in the branch.

> WE OFTEN FEAR GOING OUT ON A LIMB,
> AFRAID THAT IF IT BREAKS, WE'LL FALL.
> TRUSTING IN YOUR WINGS, NOT IN THE BRANCH,
> LIBERATES YOU TO SOAR TO WHOLE NEW HEIGHTS.

Of course, there are a gazillion books on getting fit, eating clean, sleeping tight, ageing strong, staying focused and playing your A-game. Many are well worth a read. So my purpose for this chapter is not to lay out a 23-step formula for bringing your best self to your boldest challenges, but rather to help you clarify and firm your resolve to:

- double down on the activities that expand your capacity for life, setting you up to thrive amid your challenges (and, if you're not doing any, to start)

- stop doing the activities that confine your capacity for life, working *against* you and weakening your self-trust.

Let's begin with activities and regular practices that help build your trust in your innate capacity to meet life wherever it is — to strengthen your metaphorical wings so that

a) you aren't afraid to go out on a limb and be brave with your life

b) once you're out there and you feel the bough cracking, you don't freak out because, like a bird, your trust is in your wings, not in the branch.

Building trust in your wings (that is, your innate capacity to rise above the challenges life presents) is not a one-off exercise. It requires an ongoing commitment to doing whatever supports you to be at your best — physically, mentally, emotionally and spiritually — more often. This doesn't mean you *always* feel invincible, unstoppable or ready to conquer the world. It means that when something happens that throws you off your game — you lose your job (or your partner does), your child gets sick, the market crashes, your house burns down, your lover leaves you — you're able to pick yourself up, dust yourself off, and get back to being your best self, your bravest self, sooner rather than later (or never at all).

Not to be a downer about it, but your life will never be free of pressures and problems, disappointments and difficulties. It's how you respond to them that makes the vital difference and separates those who thrive from those who don't.

Now, you might argue that some people are naturally more resilient than others. It's true. But research also shows that resilience is not an immutable trait or characteristic endowed only on the lucky few. In fact, resilience depends far less on what you have, and far more on what you do. This means that no matter your situation or personality type, you have the ability to become more resilient (once again drawing on our brain's innate neuroplasticity as discussed in the last chapter). The American Psychological Association lists a whole raft of ways people can build resilience (from building your social network to taking decisive action). What I want to focus on here is how you can cultivate the mindset required to not just to bounce back faster but to strengthen the trust you have in yourself (i.e. in those wings of yours!) so that you're not just surviving life's storms, you're thriving (laughing and dancing and celebrating life) right in the middle of them.

SMALL DAILY ACTIONS THAT FEW CAN SEE CREATE THE BIG RESULTS THAT MANY WANT.

Enter 'self-fullness'.

Self-fullness is neither self*ish* nor self*less*, both of which are really two sides of the same dysfunctional coin. Self-fullness is about prioritising daily habits and regular rituals that help you 'sharpen your saw' so that when life's problems press in and fear dials up, you have the clarity, capacity and competence you need to rise above it. After all, mastery of life is not the absence of problems, it's mastery of problems.

In recent years there's been increasing recognition of the importance of daily rituals, sometimes called 'success habits'. Do a web search of *success rituals* and you'll get 66 million suggestions (literally). Tim Ferriss has a five-step morning ritual that includes journaling, meditation and interval training. While he says he only does all five about 30 per cent of the time, even doing a few kickstarts his day on a strong footing. Oprah has a dedicated place in her home for spiritual meditation each morning before moving on with her day. Robin Sharma, author of *The 5 AM Club*, spends one hour every Sunday morning to create his 'Blueprint for a Beautiful Week', which includes reconnecting with his core values, reviewing his previous week and prioritising the one ahead. And Tony Robbins swears by his custom-tailored version of an ancient yoga breathing technique followed by a gratitude and visualisation exercise.

RESILIENCE ISN'T WHAT YOU HAVE, IT'S WHAT YOU DO. THE LITTLE THINGS YOU DO EACH DAY TO STRENGTHEN YOUR WINGS, REPEATED OFTEN, BECOME BIG THINGS.

Successful people do things that others don't. And so while some may scoff at those who get out of bed at 5 am or have quirky rituals, what these people accomplish over the course of each day, much less over their lives, is a testament to the value of these regular practices. I know when I start my day with rituals that reset my head, heart and hands in the right space, it enables me to get far more done with greater ease, less angst and more present to those around me.

During my five years living by Port Phillip Bay in Melbourne, I developed a morning run circuit that took me out onto the end of Brighton Pier, where I'd do some stretching and set my intention for the day. While the summer is an easier time to get out of bed early, it was the winter runs I found the most invigorating. They also introduced me to the 'ice-bergers': a group of men and women who swam around the pier early each morning, rain, hail or shine. So there I would be, in the chilly pre-dawn darkness, my hands in gloves and ears covered in my black fleece ear wrap (a tad more subdued than Mrs Oberg's running kit), quietly pleased with myself for braving the elements when many were still tucked warm in bed. And as I'd run out onto the pier, there would be the ice-bergers — many in their sixties and seventies — wearing nothing but a swimsuit and a waterproof headlamp, entering the cold water for their morning swim. I felt cold (and a tad wimpy) just looking at them.

One particularly dark, icy morning, when I'd taken a little longer to haul myself out of bed, I spoke to one of them, an older man who looked closer to my father's age (and my dad is in his eighties), as he was exiting the water.

'How do you get out of bed on a freezing morning like this?'

'It's not hard,' he said, 'it's often the best thing I do all day. When I don't get out here is when I feel lousy.'

What you do every day is more important than what you do every once in a while. And while braving icy winter water may not be your thing (it ain't mine), by investing time every day in actions that help you feel physically fit, emotionally centred, mentally focused and spiritually grounded you can profoundly transform your life. As Brian Tracy said, 'Successful people are simply those with successful habits.' Likewise, when life's storm waves whip up and you feel yourself being pulled under, it's your daily rituals that can help you to keep your head above the water.

IF YOUR INNER PILOT LIGHT HAS DIMMED TO A FLICKER, IT'S ON YOU TO DO WHAT IT TAKES TO DIAL IT BACK UP.

It's the times when I've felt as though life was coming at me from all directions, as it has in recent years, between derailed plans and unforeseen relocations, that I most need to double down on my rituals. While weeks can separate my journal entries when life's swinging smoothly by, when the stressors have mounted — holding the potential to trigger an emotional tsunami — my journal gets quite the workout. So too does the meditation app on my phone. (Insight Timer is my pick of them!)

Likewise, it is precisely when you feel most overwhelmed by what's coming at you, and least inclined to slow down and take a sacred pause, that you most need to step off the treadmill of frantic *doing* and invest time in who you are *being*.

These are often also the times you're most tempted to scroll mindlessly through your social media feed or go shopping or down a bottle of wine or eat a gallon of ice cream without actually tasting it. All good for distraction, but not good for your soul or stress levels.

Of course, booking yourself into a five-star wellness resort for a week might be nice at times like this. But, let's face it, that's not an option for most folks. What *is* an option is taking an hour (or even twenty minutes) to get your head and heart in the right space to handle everything else better.

Perhaps as you're reading this now you're feeling on top of the world. If so, well done you and enjoy this moment. But if not, then I invite you to think about a few things you could do that would help you feel calmer, stronger and more positive in any way. In 'Prioritise what empowers', I've included a few questions to help you think about what more you could be doing for yourself so you can handle everything else better, particularly in the times when trusting your wings is mission critical.

THE MORE LIFE IS DEMANDING OF YOU, THE MORE
CRUCIAL IT IS TO RECHARGE AND RESET
FOR WHAT'S COMING NEXT.

PRIORITISE WHAT EMPOWERS

Your ability to bounce back when life hits you is not about whether you were born as a resilient person. It's about the decisions you make day in, day out, to do what helps you to be more resilient. Moving the needle on how you show up and rise up is entirely within your control. So, what can you do right now to bring your best self to your biggest challenges?

Physically

Our 'earth suits' carry us through life, yet often we neglect to nurture them adequately. You cannot expect your body to keep up with the life you want to live if you're neglecting it, not eating what nourishes you and consuming too much of what doesn't. Same again if you're neglecting to get sufficient rest or letting your muscles wither. What activities **re-energise** you, and

refuel your stamina, strength and physical wellbeing? Does how you eat, how often you exercise and how much you sleep set you up to thrive? If not, what needs to change? Research finds that exercising three times a week has the equivalent effect of anti-depressant or anti-anxiety drugs. Building physical muscles helps to build psychological ones. The two are inextricably linked.

Mentally

You have the intellectual ability to succeed in meaningful endeavours in your life. However in today's age of distraction, we have to be careful to stay focused on the 'vital few' lest we waste our time and mental horsepower on the 'trivial many'. What practices clear your mental clutter and **refocus** you on your top priorities? If you're often distracted, what can you do to **reprioritise** your schedule to make the most of the hours in your day?

Emotionally

The quality of our emotions dictates the quality of our lives. It's why the strongest predictor of success is not IQ, it's EQ. Learning to manage your emotional state is pivotal to your happiness, health and staying resilient when challenges press in. Where do you need to own your feelings more fully so they don't own you? What activities **reconnect** you to your sense of optimism, confidence and connection and **reframe** your perspective to help you lighten up and laugh more? How can you incorporate more of them into each day? Who do you need to spend more time with, and who can you minimise time with? (More on this in chapter 10.)

Spiritually

In its simplest form, spirituality is about being connected to something greater than yourself. What activities help you **recharge** your spirit, **realign** to what brings you the greatest meaning and **reignite** a deeper sense of your purpose? And when you feel down on yourself and on your life, how does the most loving, kind place within you **respond** to your small self? If what you read, watch and do in your down time is not connecting you to the wisdom of your true self but fuelling the fears and egoic insecurities of your small self, decide to do something to tip the balance the other way.

Author John Maxwell wrote, 'You'll never change your life until you change something you do daily. The secret of your success is found in your daily routine.' Yet prioritising time in your day to 'sharpen your saw' is often at the mercy of 101 less-important tasks. So make a commitment to yourself to do more of what strengthens you and brings out your best, and less of what doesn't. Schedule activities in. Then treat the commitments you make to yourself with every bit as much integrity — *or more!* — as you would if you were making them to other people.

In short, you become what you repeatedly do. Not what you think you *should* do. Or what you say you *will* do. But what you *actually* do. And as management guru Peter Drucker once said, 'If you want something new, you've got to stop doing something old.'

BUILDING YOUR CAPACITY FOR LIFE ISN'T JUST ABOUT DOING MORE OF WHAT STRENGTHENS YOU; IT'S ABOUT *NOT* DOING WHAT MAKES YOU WEAKER.

Strengthening your wings is also about consciously spending less time on activities that make you more anxious and less grounded in yourself. Toxic relationships. Toxic media. Time-wasting habits. Talking yourself down. Talking others down. Staying up too late and mistreating your 'earth-suit' too often.

This isn't to say that it's not beneficial to spend time doing nothing and being what Type A's might call 'unproductive'; you need to regularly mentally disengage with the world in order to re-engage with it more constructively. Rather, it's about being intentional in your disengagement. Downtime you plan for is not wasted time; it's the downtime you *don't* plan for (like spending 30 minutes scrolling Instagram) that is doing you no favours.

Even devoting five minutes to strengthen yourself in some way — visualising your day going well, reading something uplifting, writing in your gratitude journal, doing a short mindfulness exercise, mentally counting your blessings — can make a profound difference to your mindset and set you up for an entirely different day.

The good news is that you build good habits the same way you build bad ones — with practice. It's just that good habits require a level of discipline that bad habits don't. Being intentional is the golden ticket!

Set your alarm and get out of bed half an hour early to spend quiet time in reflection, or to map out your day or read something that elevates your thinking and ignites your spirit.

Spend 30 minutes every day to stretch or strengthen your body.

Place a gratitude journal by your bed and take ten minutes at night to do the 'Five to Thrive' exercise in the previous chapter.

Take a sacred pause three times during your day to do a very simple breathing exercise to reground you in your (true) self.

Consume only books and media that nourish you in some way. (If you're reading this, you're a step ahead already!)

Schedule a daily 'digital detox' window to unplug from your devices and plug in to yourself and those around you.

And if you don't get to do these things every day, do not underestimate the impact of the things you do *most* days — journaling, communing with nature, listening to music, appreciating those around you or doing something loving for yourself! To paraphrase Johann Goethe, never let those things that matter most be at the mercy of those that matter least.

When I moved to Singapore, my morning runs were replaced by morning swims as I just found the humidity too oppressive to enjoy running. But wherever I am, I always prioritise some form of exercise to wake up my body, ideally also being outdoors in nature as that has the double benefit of fuelling my spirit as well. When I'm travelling for work, sometimes the best I can manage is ten minutes stretching in my hotel room. While I don't nearly qualify as a hard core fitness freak, I just know that starting my day by moving this earth suit of mine sets me up for a better day.

Equally important to strengthening your wings and maximising your 'capacity for life' is staying connected to your intuition, which I define as a deeper source of wisdom that is woven through the physical, mental, emotional and spiritual dimensions of our lives. Uninhibited by our biases and judgements, wired only to perception, our intuition gives us access to an internal guidance system, that operates beyond our conscious thought, that is always working for our highest good. You may have felt it over the years in the form of a quirky urge, a weird inkling you couldn't quite put your finger on, or a deep inexplicable knowing that 'this just feels right' (or maybe 'this feels wrong!'). By learning to tap into your intuition you can deepen your trust in your own judgement and, with it, your faith that whatever happens around you, you can figure it out.

YOUR INTUITION IS YOUR INNER SAGE, HELPING YOU DISCERN REAL THREATS FROM IMAGINARY ONES. TUNE IN TO WHAT IT'S TRYING TO TELL YOU.

Often when we are feeling overwhelmed with life or unsure of the best way forward, we try to intellectualise our way out of it. I've seen people come up with all sorts of elaborate spreadsheets, with different weightings on various dimensions, creating a rubric to optimise their decision making. It's not that there's anything wrong with critical analysis, but when we try to rely solely on it we cut ourselves off from a higher, intuitive source of guidance that transcends anything we can intellectually figure out. As Albert Einstein once said, 'The intuitive mind is a sacred gift and the rational mind is a faithful servant. We have created a society that honors the servant and has forgotten the gift.'

Our ability to access this 'sacred gift' of our intuition relies on quieting the noise that often drowns it out. There are various ways people do this: meditation, prayer, music, journaling, sitting quietly in nature. You might try writing a letter to your 'true self' or to your future self — you at a ripe old age with all those years of learning under your belt — asking them for advice.

Journaling is one useful method for accessing our 'inner sage'. My own personal practice is writing down what I'm toiling with and then asking a higher source of wisdom – my own inner sage – for guidance. What you call your inner sage or Higher Power doesn't matter. Personally, I just call it God because, I believe, as Brené Brown wrote in *The Gifts of Imperfection*, that 'God lives within us, not above us'. So I generally begin my journal entries with a little vent and recap of the day or week's news, and then I write, *So God, what do you want me to know?* Then I just let my pen flow. What appears on the page tends to clear the muddy mental waters, quell my rumination and restore my clarity and reconnect me to my true self. It doesn't come from an intellectual place, but a spiritual one.

Here's what landed on my page not so long ago. You might want to insert your own name at the top ... after all, the same wisdom that lives in me lives in all of us, so perhaps these words will also speak to you also.

Dear Margie

Yes, these are challenging times. But just because life is uncertain doesn't mean it's not ripe with opportunity for you to learn and grow and blossom in ways you might never do otherwise.

So fear not. Rather keep faith that you are exactly where you're intended to be; that there is a higher order at play beyond what you can see.

And when your doubts grow loud, remember to trust in yourself, your gifts and the inherent goodness of life.

You are not inadequate in any way. You are not being left behind. You are not off course. And you are not lost.

Not at all.

Not while you pursue what lights you up.

Not while you do what you know is right.

Not while you act with the courage you wish for in others.

Embrace today for all it holds, embrace yourself for all you are, and when your fears rise up, embrace them too.

It is all part of your journey ... your unfolding ... your becoming.

All necessary to prepare you for what lies ahead.

And what lies ahead will fill your heart beyond anything left behind.

Go in grace. Go in peace. Go in faith.

Go be present to those you love.

Go do what today requires.

You know what it is.

You've got this.

And I've got you.

Always.

God

This ritual may sound a little 'woo woo' to some — particularly committed atheists. However these 'love letters' tap into a wisdom beyond my own intellectual reasoning and always serve to keep the lower-order motivations of my small self in check, reset my highest intentions and bolster the trust I have in my ability to handle whatever comes my way — one day, one hour, and sometimes one minute at a time.

So I took the risk of sharing my personal journaling ritual to encourage you to create one for yourself. Research shows that the practice of journaling helps us process emotions and gain objectivity when we're lacking it. As I will share in chapter 10, research also shows having some form of spiritual belief system helps people cope better with adversity. It's my own grounded theory that combining the two has a magnified impact!

If this doesn't sound like your thing, that's okay. However if you've found yourself feeling continually flat or fearful, negative or upset in any way, don't keep doing more of what's already not working in the vain hope that at some point it will. Hope isn't a strategy and wishful thinking is just that.

Instead, try this little experiment with yourself. Just write a note to your inner sage, asking that wisest part of you what it would like you to know right now, particularly regarding a specific challenge you're facing or decision you're wrangling with. You might even include how challenged you are by the very concept that there's a 'wise self' on tap within you 24/7. Like I said, just play with this as an experiment. Worst case scenario is you waste a little ink. Best case, you strengthen a line of communication with a source of wisdom that's got your back. What's to lose?

THE MORE YOU CALL ON THE HIGHEST TRUTH
WITHIN YOURSELF, THE MORE IT COMES FORTH.
YOU KNOW THE TRUTH FROM
THE WAY IT FEELS.

There is no telling what 'return on investment' you will get from being more intentional every day to prioritise what empowers you. So if you do nothing else, what about making a commitment in the day ahead that will strengthen your wings?

The best outcomes tend to flow out of the smallest daily actions. So do yourself a favour, set yourself up to get really clear about what small things you will do for yourself. Things that will help you to ...

Focus your time on the 'vital few' priorities that matter most?

Sharpen your strengths and cultivate your gifts?

Re-energise you to pursue your boldest life?

Infuse deeper gratitude for all the good in your life right now?

Dim down your doubts and ignite your passion?

Build deeper, richer connections to those around you?

Make you laugh, lighten up and let go of the small stuff?

Nourish your body and set yourself up to age strong?

Write them down, schedule them in, and do it. If you notice any difference, any at all, then repeat again tomorrow. And of course if one of them happens to include going for a jog in turquoise shorts with a neon terry-towelling headband, I suggest smiling while you run. Because I have a suspicion people may be smiling at you.

'Genius
is talent
set on fire
by courage.'

Henry van Dyke

6
Use Your Gifts
Trust your talents and play to your strengths

'CQ, CQ, CQ DX, Dingo 502 callin' to see who's out there,' my brother Frank would say into his CB radio handset.

'G'day there Dingo 502, comin' through loud and clear,' a crackly voice would respond from the beyond.

These conversations, about nothing in particular (at least to my ears), would go on for hours and hours, night after night, often in lieu of Frank doing his homework.

Frank loved his CB radio. He loved *every* radio. In fact, we were hard pressed to find a few square inches in his bedroom that weren't covered in paraphernalia from the many radios, televisions and telephones he would dismantle. One time he even climbed to the top of a huge old peppercorn tree next to our house to install his own oversized homemade antenna (which, once discovered by our younger brothers, Steve and Pete, became their new favourite object for target practice). Frank drew enormous satisfaction from pulling apart multiple radios to reassemble their pieces into a better one. It all fascinated him.

Me on the other hand ... not so much. In fact, I had little interest in understanding how sound could be transmitted from one place to another, miles apart. And to be honest, I still don't. (As long as the button works, I'm good!)

Years later, when digital technology began to replace analogue, I asked Frank to explain what that meant. He did. Many times. But it wasn't until I actually started to use an iPhone that I began to grasp what he'd been telling me years before.

If society were reliant on me alone for technological advancement, we'd still be using smoke signals and the Pony Express.

Frank's brain, on the other hand, is wired to understand the intricacies of telecommunications. He has the gift of the gadget. So it delighted me when, a few years out of high school after training as an electrical technician, he decided to go to university to become a telecommunications engineer. And it never surprises me now when people say that he's a very good one; it was there from the beginning.

Frank claims his CB radio network was an early form of social media, and that he was a man ahead of his time, 'making friends' over the airwaves with people he hardly knew or might never meet.

We are all born with latent talents and gifts — sharpened and unsharpened. They develop into strengths with consistent practice over time.

It's fair to say that Frank has developed a strength in understanding telecommunications technology. He could spend hours explaining to you the difference between 4G and 5G or how the Apple Watch is set up to make mobile calls. In fact he designed the solution for the iWatch to access Australia's largest mobile phone network (and which — small sister brag — he later heard was the most successful solution globally).

While I don't share my brother's gifts when it comes to technology (in fact, I'm a bit of a chaos agent when it comes to tech), I do have my own. Cultivating these gifts is a work in progress, but what I've learnt is that it's far more energising (and less disheartening) to work from my strengths than to spend any more than the minimal time needed to shore up my weaknesses.

Alas, if you spot a typo on these pages, my apologies. Attention to detail is not a strength, so I outsource apostrophe placement to those with a penchant for it. Same for home styling, growing plants and gift wrapping ... definitely not my sweet spots. Hence why I've come to regard these areas as opportunities to practise abundance: I outsource, delegate or order in.

A few years back I spoke at the same event as Jim Clifton, Chairman and CEO of Gallup. Gallup do a lot of surveys, one of which has been to identify core 'signature strengths'. Jim shared how organisational skills were not one of his and how he learnt early in his career — after a series of organisational mishaps — to surround himself with very organised people.

Richard Branson shared a similar approach. He doesn't thrive in the details and isn't great with computers. So he outsources to people who are far stronger in these domains, leaving him to work from his entrepreneurial strengths and flair for building Virgin's global business and social impact.

DO MORE OF WHAT LIGHTS YOU UP (AND LESS OF WHAT DOESN'T)!

Of course we aren't all in a position to outsource the tasks we don't much like. However, when you are intentional about investing as much time as you can right now (even if it's not as much as you'd like) in your own personal 'sweet spot' you'll find yourself moving forward, faster than you ever could by trying to shore up a weakness. As I wrote in *Make Your Mark,* your sweet spot is the intersection between what it is *you do well* (nurturing your talents and building your strengths) and whatever it is that *you love to do* (because it lights you up and gives you meaning, self-expression and connection, deepening your sense of your unique value).

Research backs this up. When you invest energy sharpening your strengths and expressing your talents, it not only enhances your general sense of wellbeing, but it builds your confidence to take on even larger and more meaningful challenges in the future. Research from Gallup found that people who use their strengths are three times more likely to report an excellent quality of life. (Alarmingly, that Gallup also found people spend 80 per cent of their time at work trying to shore up their weaknesses!) When you harness your gifts and play from your strengths, it wards off doubt, bolsters belief and produces better outcomes. In fact, Gallup's research has found that the most impactful lever in transforming entire organisational cultures — and improving bottom line outcomes — is a strengths-based approach to management.

Civil rights leader Howard Thurman once advised, 'Don't ask what the world needs. Ask what makes you come alive, and go do it. Because what the world needs is people who have come alive.' Which begs the question:

What makes you feel most alive?

Some people can easily name their greatest strengths. Yet many of us struggle (often because we're so preoccupied with our weaknesses!). If you're not sure of yours, try asking five people around you what they think are your top five strengths. I've assigned this as homework to clients numerous times and it's never failed to be illuminating and affirming.

My friend Michelle McQuaid became an expert in building strengths-based workplaces after getting stuck in a major career rut. It took her by surprise. After all, she'd landed a highly sought-after position as global brand manager for a large consulting firm and was living in Manhattan. Yet as the months wore on, she found herself feeling increasingly unhappy and disillusioned with her high-status, high-salary, big-brand corporate gig. It took her a while to realise what was out of sync. And then it dawned on her: she was no longer spending her days doing what drew on her strengths and brought her the most satisfaction. So she decided to be very intentional and make sure she spent at least ten minutes a day doing the things she most loved until she could find a pathway into a new career where she would be able to spend a whole lot more time than that. As Michelle's research has since verified, when we spend time each day doing what we do best, we're more productive, our stress levels go down and our wellbeing goes up.

PERHAPS YOUR TIREDNESS ISN'T FROM DOING TOO MUCH. PERHAPS THE REAL PROBLEM IS THAT YOU'RE DOING TOO LITTLE OF WHAT FUELS YOU.

'Amid the whirlwind of modern life,' wrote Sister Joan Chittister, one of the greatest theologians of our time, 'we risk the loss of life itself.' So be intentional with your hours, with what you do with your talents and time. Amid the hurly burly of priorities and pressures, make sure you incorporate into your days things that draw on your strengths, nurture your talents and make you feel more alive, not less so. And if you often feel tired and running on empty, ask yourself whether it's because you're doing too much, or if it's because you're doing too little of what fills you up and ignites new energy within you.

In case it isn't yet obvious, I have a deep passion for empowering people to become the fullest and most fearless version of who they can be. Over the course of any given year, I meet hundreds of other people who also feel called to empower others. Coaches, therapists, speakers, advocates, counsellors, performance psychologists, academics, teachers, healers, event planners, writers, performers ... even the occasional reformed attorney. All of us get lit up by helping others light up, yet we all draw on different strengths and life experiences to do that.

Some people scale up their operations. They set up franchises and 'train the trainers'. Some create large online platforms that harness AI technology. Some, like me, write and speak to large audiences and facilitate groups, while others work exclusively one on one with clients. Some write music. Some film daily videos on Instagram and others lead adventure tours that require complete unplugging from technology. Some run non-profits, others large companies.

THERE IS NO ONE FORMULA FOR SUCCESS. BUT EVERY FORMULA INCLUDES TRUSTING IN YOUR UNIQUE GIFTS AND FORGING YOUR UNIQUE PATH.

Those who are truly thriving in their careers and life are those who work from their strengths and forge their own unique path, rather than trying to copy that of someone else. When I was just starting to speak publicly, I made the mistake of trying to imitate the style of other speakers. It neither felt quite right nor worked very well as it always felt a little incongruent with who I am and my own unique personality. It took time to really trust in my own strengths and style. Yet it taught me a valuable lesson: trust *your* gifts, own *your* strengths, and don't assume what works for someone else is right for you.

Sure, there are things you can learn from the masters in your field, but there is nothing as powerful as simply trusting in *your own* gifts and forging *your own* path in *your own* way. I've long since given up trying to incorporate anything high-tech into my programs because, as I've learnt through plenty of trial and error, my gift is connecting from the heart space — and using anything more than simple technology gets in the way of that.

The same principle applies to you. Sure, talk to experts, watch and learn from those excelling in whatever arena you aspire to succeed in, but never give any one person the authority to determine what is right for you. Rather, notice what they do that resonates for you, and then draw on your observations to hone your own game in your own way. Let your own truth be your highest authority, not anyone else's.

DON'T COMPARE. EVERY MINUTE YOU SPEND ENVYING ANOTHER'S STRENGTHS IS A MINUTE YOU AREN'T MAKING THE MOST OF YOUR OWN.

Just because a turkey can't fly doesn't make it a failed bird. Which is why focusing on using your unique gifts rather than trying to copy those of others is your golden ticket. We aren't all made to climb trees or teach children or design buildings or write music or launch start ups, or run billion-dollar businesses. Yet every single one of us has a unique combination of strengths, gifts, talents and knowledge from the 'school of life' that we are called to share with the world. When we get caught up in the ego trap of comparing our strengths and talents and place in the world with those of others, it dilutes our ability to fully harness our strengths. Comparisons are the 'thief of joy' because they rob us from being truly present to (and trusting of) the gifts within us and always leave us feeling 'less than' in some way.

I'm not as charismatic or quick-witted as him.

I'm not as creative or credentialled as her.

I'll never be as good at (fill-in-the-blank) as they are.

For all you know, others may be looking enviously at you, hostage to their own comparisons. Wishing they had your eye for design or knack for numbers or entrepreneurial flair or gift of the gab.

What others are doing with their gifts is *on them*. What you are doing with your gifts is *on you*. No-one else. So focus on what you're good at, not on what you'll never excel at.

My friend Sarah can whip up a feast for a horde of people with humour and ease. What a gift that's been to me on many occasions. But she'd be the first to say she's the last person to ask for fashion advice.

My own husband, Andrew, is brilliant at cutting through complexity and seeing patterns amid (seeming) chaos. He thrives leading change and finding smarter solutions to commercial problems and tapping the potential in those around him (I'm one of many who's been the fortunate recipient of this!). Yet he has earned a reputation among our kids for his 'fusion cooking': throwing whatever random food he can find in the back recesses of the pantry or far corners of the fridge into a large pot, adding a tin of peeled tomatoes and some soy sauce, serving it up on rice or pasta and hoping it's edible (so far, no luck — though he would argue otherwise).

YOU CAN'T TAKE CREDIT FOR YOUR GIFTS. ALL YOU CAN TAKE CREDIT FOR IS WHAT YOU DO WITH THEM.

I'm sure if we sat down for a cup of tea, I'd soon learn about what you're good at and what lights you up. While I have no idea what one-of-a-kind combination of gifts you have, I'm absolutely certain that only when you decide to use them in ways that serve the world, and let go of trying to shore up your weaknesses or be like anyone else, can you ever achieve what you're capable of or enjoy the fulfilment you seek. As the saying goes, 'If you judge a fish by its ability to climb a tree, it will spend its whole life believing it's stupid.'

When I was growing up my mother had a sideboard filled with fine bone china, crockery and platters she'd received as engagement and wedding gifts. She explained their year-round shelving by saying that if she used them, they'd almost certainly end up chipped or broken.

It was true. Yet it left me wondering: what's the point of these gifts if not to use and enjoy them? The same thought has crossed my mind on the few occasions I've visited someone's home (often from a generation or two beyond me) to see their furniture wrapped in plastic (often still left on from the factory), to protect it from wear and tear. What's the point of buying lovely furniture if you have to sit on plastic wrap?

Your natural gifts are no different.

You can play it safe and keep them shelved away to avoid ever having your pride chipped. But at what cost? It just deprives you and everyone else of reaping the beauty and benefits your gifts might otherwise hold.

If you have a gift, it's for a reason: to be used up, shared around, leveraged fully. As Rachel Hollis says, 'Talents and skills are like any other living things ... they can't grow in the dark.'

GIFTS ARE MADE TO BE SHARED, NOT SHELVED AWAITING PERFECT CONDITIONS. NOT USING YOUR GIFTS EXACTS A HIDDEN TAX ON THE EMOTIONAL BALANCE SHEET OF YOUR LIFE.

What's more, not using your gift, leaving it on the shelf beside my mother's bone china, actually comes at a cost you rarely see right away. It's not a case of 'oh well, that's just too bad' and off you go on your merry way. Nope: when you fail to use the gifts, strengthen the talents and develop the strengths you were born with through no doing of your own, it incurs a hidden tax on the emotional balance sheet of your life.

Of course, some people never have the opportunity to use their gifts. Throughout history, millions of people have lived their entire lives without access to the education or opportunities to develop their gifts. Some still don't.

But chances are, if you're reading this now, you are not one of those people.

You may be wondering what 'tax' you are paying for not sharing your gifts, or at least not as fully as you know you could be.

Perhaps it's a lingering sense of restlessness. Something in your life just feels amiss, out of alignment or harmony in some way. It's hard to put your finger on it, but you just sense, in quiet moments or the wee hours of the night, that there is something you're not doing that you need to be doing. Something that is not going to be brought into the world, that will remain undone, because you have not given yourself permission to do it, for fear you'll be inadequate for the task.

Of course, it's not just restlessness you have to contend with. It's all the other emotions that flow from it. Sadness. Depression. Discontent. Resentment. Anger. Self-pity. Blame (because, of course it's always more convenient to point the finger at someone else). And, as life passes by, sometimes it's deep, lingering regrets for the unlived life within you. Sadly, far too many people live in this state, leading, as Thoreau wrote so poetically, 'lives of quiet desperation' and going to their grave with their song still inside them.

To avoid such feelings, many choose to numb and distract themselves. They get very busy being very busy, coming up with an array of highly reasonable and creative rationalisations for why they are not doing that thing that they know, in their heart of hearts, they feel called to do.

Hopefully you are not one of them. Because, for a while, numbing works ... at least on some level. Ask any serial drinker, gambler, sexaholic. We *Homo sapiens* may do some pretty daft things but we always do them for some payoff. The question you have to ask yourself is whether what you are getting from your current choices is worth what you are giving up. Not trusting in your unique strengths comes at a cost — affecting the state of your heart, your health, your relationships and your day-by-day, moment-by-moment experience of being alive.

So be careful you don't get hoodwinked by your own confirmation bias and look only for the evidence that supports your story that you are not gifted for anything. Because the truth is, that's utterly untrue. Totally, utterly, completely ... false.

YOU DO NOT LACK THE RESOURCES TO DO MORE OF WHATEVER IT IS THAT LIGHTS YOU UP. YOU HAVE JUST LACKED THE RESOLVE ... UNTIL NOW.

That said, don't go off half-cocked.

Doing more of what makes you come alive does not mean you must immediately quit your job to paint watercolours full time to sell at weekend crafts markets. Nor does it mean you abrogate all your responsibilities and move to Nashville to try your luck at turning your yodeling talent into a country music career. (Though of course, this doesn't mean you can't!)

It just means that you start finding ways of incorporating more of whatever it is you *love* to do, what you are *good* at doing, what you feel *called* to do, into your life as it is today. And if you truly do feel called to the life of an artist, use this time to rework your finances and re-engineer your life to set yourself up for a new future. You're smart. You can figure it out. You just have to be creative and committed to finding ways of doing this without compromising your other core values. Like paying your bills or feeding your kids.

Take Tania Brown. Tania has a finance background and is working for a large international tech company and enjoys the challenges of her role. Yet she also has a gift for solving problems and an entrepreneurial flair. Over the years she's often felt frustrated by the lack of stylish laptop bags for women. While she wasn't about to quit her job to become a laptop bag designer, she wanted to use her creativity and understanding of financial modelling to build an ecommerce business and produce her own line of beautiful hand-crafted leather laptop bags for professional women, which she launched under the brand Jacq Leigh. I happen to be the proud owner of one such red leather bag, and I share this because every time I head out with my sleek red bag (sometimes even with matching lipstick!), it makes me feel good. In fact, I'm looking at it right now as I type.

There is no shortage of opportunities for anyone to use their gifts and sharpen their strengths in ways that make them come alive and light up others; there's just a shortage of resolve.

RISK BEING FOUND OUT AS A TALENTLESS FRAUD. THAT'S HOW YOU EXPOSE THE REAL IMPOSTER: THE DOUBTS IN YOUR OWN HEAD.

A pattern I've observed in many people (and which I admit is still a 'work in progress' for myself), is the tendency to dismiss, discount and downplay our gifts and strengths. This is one of the key dynamics that contributes to 'imposter syndrome'. If you're unfamiliar with the term, it's basically the phenomenon of people feeling like a fraud, undeserving of their success and anxious about when the world will cotton on to the fact that they not as capable or deserving of accolades as everyone thinks.

If you have ever felt this way, you're not alone! It's estimated that 70 per cent of people will experience imposter syndrome at some point in their lives. And of course, apart from the odd serial narcissist, no-one is immune from moments of feeling as though they're not as capable as people think they are. Even the most gifted and accomplished people, whom you might assume would be beyond any anxiety about living up to expectations, can sometimes fear they'll be 'found out' as a fraud.

Starbucks's Howard Schultz said in an interview with *The New York Times* about being a CEO,

> *Very few people, whether you've been in that job before or not, get into the seat and believe today that they are now qualified to be the CEO. They're not going to tell you that, but it's true.*

Likewise, Nobel Laureate Maya Angelou once said,

> *I have written eleven books, but each time I think, 'uh oh, they're going to find out now. I've run a game on everybody, and they're going to find me out.'*

Similarly, during her time heading up the World Health Organization, Margaret Chan said,

> *There are an awful lot of people out there who think I'm an expert. How do these people believe all this about me? I'm so much aware of all the things I don't know.*

In fact, it seems that the more we know about any particular field, the more we know about how much we *don't* know, and the higher the bar we set for ourselves. Debra, a former client and high-profile litigation attorney, once told me how she often feels people think she knows more than she does, particularly in the area of law in which she has the strongest reputation.

Perhaps you also tend to devalue your strengths or, when you are being praised for something you've done well that's drawn upon them, you tend to brush off the accolades and downplay the strengths rather than appreciate them.

But again, what you appreciate appreciates. The more you embrace your talents and cultivate your strengths, the more you'll value them and the greater value they will create for others. They'll also raise your performance. As the study I mentioned in chapter 2 found, priming ourselves to focus on our top strengths and skills can lift our performance. So if you're feeling inadequate, take just five minutes to jot down all the things you're good at and the accomplishments that bring you the most pride. Once you get the juices flowing, you'll realise that you have not fully appreciated the many strengths and skills you have to contribute.

THERE IS NOTHING HOLY IN DIMINISHING YOURSELF. HUMILITY IS A VIRTUE BUT TALKING YOURSELF DOWN SERVES NO-ONE.

A few years ago, I got to spend a few days with author Marianne Williamson, an author I'd long admired who has since become a friend as well as entered into the political arena (more on that later.) Upon meeting her, she asked me what I did.

'Oh, I'm an author,' I replied, then added, a little self-consciously, 'but not near as successful as you.'

'Got it, you're an author,' she said, in a tone that emphasised how I should have just ended my reply at 'author'. 'You Australians are very charming, and your humility can be quite endearing,' she added, though I sensed a 'but' was coming ... 'But there is nothing holy in diminishing yourself.'

The truth of her words penetrated right through me. She was right: self-deprecation may be a well-worn habit born from my childhood fear of appearing 'up myself', but there is nothing noble about belittling oneself. As I write in the next chapter, which is dedicated to women, diminishing ourselves safeguards against the risk of being perceived as arrogant, conceited or too self-assured. Far better to pull ourselves down before anyone else can, right? Well, no, not right. Because while we should be thoughtful about how we appear to others, any time we let fear of judgement call the shots, we sell ourselves short and do everyone a disservice.

Wind the clock forward a few years: I visited Marianne's home to interview her for my podcast. She enquired when it would be published and after telling her 'September', I added self-consciously, 'Of course, I don't have anywhere near the platform of Oprah.'

Aaargggh ... old habits die hard!

'Stop it,' she said, with the fierceness I've grown to admire in her. 'Has Oprah had four children? No. Has Oprah lived all over the world? No. So stop with all this Oprah nonsense. It doesn't serve you, Margie, and you owe it to yourself to stop saying things that diminish what you've done or what you are intending to do. Truly, Margie, will you do that?'

'I'll try,' I replied, feeling like a kid who didn't get the lesson the first time round.

'Don't *try*,' she said, staring at me the way I do at my kids when they say they will 'try' to clean their room. 'Just stop it.'

And so I have.

(Except the days I forget; there's been a few. But then I figure they just offer me a chance to strengthen my self-compassion muscles!)

TOO OFTEN WE TALK UP OUR WEAKNESS, TALK DOWN OUR STRENGTHS AND DWELL ON ALL THE REASONS *WHY NOT*. DON'T ARGUE FOR YOUR LIMITATIONS, ARGUE FOR YOUR POSSIBILITIES.

Too often we argue *for* our limitations, talk *up* our weakness and talk *down* our strengths. This isn't about living in denial of what we need to work at or how we have fallen short. Rather, it's about owning the things that you *are* good at and the times that you do manage to kick it out of the park. Or just kick anything!

This isn't about over-inflating yourself, being conceited or 'stuck up' (the ultimate offence in the social environment of my Aussie childhood ... and still now). It's about simply owning your strengths and, even if you're thinking it, not verbally devaluing your accomplishments with, 'Oh, anyone could have done it.' Because, truth is, 'anyone' didn't do it. You did!

So if you sometimes feel you 'just got lucky' with where you've landed, then do this little self-audit. Take a few minutes to write down a list of every personally significant goal you've achieved and obstacle you've overcome over the last ten years. Or if that's too much of a stretch, try the last three. Or one! I'll wager that you brought a whole lot of strengths to the table that you aren't giving yourself the credit you're due.

We often take our strengths for granted, normalising what comes easily to us. People who are great with mental math can be baffled by how others can struggle with it. And those who can strike up a conversation with anyone, anywhere, often don't get why others find it so hard. When something comes naturally for us, it's all too easy to think 'but anyone could have done it.' But here's the deal: they didn't, and you did. So own it. Maybe you're a little more gifted than you give yourself credit for. Maybe a lot more!

But what's that you say?

I'm far from the most gifted person. Other people have similar gifts to me. Other people have used their gifts to accomplish pretty impressive stuff.

Good for them! But what others are doing with their gifts is, in the grand scheme of your life, utterly irrelevant. What *is* relevant is what you are doing with yours. Because, as gifted as other people around you might be, no-one, bar no-one, is in the position to use *your* gifts the way *you* are. We each have our own unique brand of brilliance and it's our personal responsibility to figure out how to hone it and do good with it. As the Roman statesman Marcus Tullius Cicero wrote, 'Not for ourselves alone are we born.'

We each arrive into the world with a sacred contract — to use our gifts to serve the world in some way. When we fail to do so, it not only fails to honour the innate brilliance of who we are, but it also does a profound disservice to all those whose lives could have been enriched had our gifts not been left dormant.

Of course, this does not mean that you will always land on your feet. Not everything you touch will turn to gold. Not everyone around you will value your gifts or celebrate your success. And the courage you summon to use your strengths and share your gifts offers no guarantee of fortune or fame as the 'world best' at whatever you want to do.

WHEN YOU CELEBRATE YOUR SMALL WINS AND CRADLE YOUR STRONG MOMENTS YOU MAGNIFY THEIR IMPACT AND BOLSTER YOUR SELF-BELIEF.

But this is not about being *the* best *in* the world. It's about giving *your* best *to* the world. More important still, the more often you give your best (whether or not it's even remotely close to world class) and do whatever brings out your best, the better person you will become. And the best part? The more you use your gifts to help others get what they want, the more you'll get what you want.

Remember what I said in chapter 4 about how the negative moments (like that one little bit of criticism) tend to stick to you while the positive moments (and all those words of praise) roll right off? Well, since you're wired to cradle your negative moments, you have to be equally deliberate to cradle your positive ones. This means not brushing off or racing past the small wins and steps forward. So set an intention to be more present to the tasks you *did* excel at, the contribution you *did* make, the challenge you *did* overcome. Not all those you did *not*.

Stop. Savour the moment. Appreciate the progress. Receive the praise. Internalise your success. Celebrate the win.

And then, and *only* then, move on.

FORGET TRYING TO ADD IN WHAT GOD LEFT OUT. RATHER DRAW OUT WHAT GOD LEFT IN.

Someone once told me not to try outsmarting God by trying to put in what God left out. Far smarter is to draw out what God left in. This means paying someone else to post my podcasts so I can spend more time thinking about what I'd like to say in them. Or say to you now, right here.

What does it mean for you? And what would you be doing if you were doing more to honour what 'God left in'?

As D. H. Lawrence once wrote, 'Men are not free when they are doing just what they like. Men are only free when they are doing what their deepest [true] self likes.'

Just for today, decide that you are going to insert into your busy schedule more 'strong moments' that make you feel more alive and draw on your gifts. Then tomorrow, do the same. And each time you do — stop, savour, appreciate, receive, celebrate.

You may always struggle to fully trust in your gifts. A small part of you may always fear being uncovered as a fraud. (I'm still working on this myself.) However, by committing to using your strengths in ways that serve not just yourself, but benefit the world, you will come to realise the only imposter you ever had to worry about was the doubting critic in your head.

'We women hold ourselves back. We think we aren't experienced enough when in fact we are.'

Kathy Calvin

7

Dear Women

Stop selling yourself short and talking yourself down

We are woman, hear us roar!

Some days.

On others ... not so much. More likely, those around us hear us talking ourselves down, second-guessing our decisions, dwelling on our mistakes or just worrying about when people will finally cotton on to the fact that we don't know as much as they think or are less deserving than they thought. I'm fairly confident that's not just me.

When it comes to self-doubt and internal recrimination, we women reign supreme.

The question is, at what cost? To ourselves, to the children we're raising, the organisations we work for and the world at large?

Hillary Clinton once said that women are the greatest reservoir of untapped potential in the world. It's true. We are. Despite all the progress that's been made, we're still such a long way from sitting at the decision-making tables in numbers equal to men.

There are many external barriers that tilt the playing field and steepen the climb for women. Unconscious bias. Unaffordable childcare. Inflexible workplaces. Caregiver expectations. Too few sponsors. Too many gendered 'think manager, think male' norms that create backlash for women who violate them.

Yet some of the biggest hurdles we must still contend with are the invisible barriers inside our own heads. Wherever I've travelled in the world, time and time again I meet incredibly capable women with so much to offer who doubt themselves too much, back themselves too little, and sell themselves too short. Perhaps you are one of them. Perhaps you hold yourself back before anyone else ever gets the chance to.

Of course, this doesn't mean women aren't trying; far from it.

We're trying hard. Ridiculously hard. The so called 'emancipation' of women from the first wave of feminism has given Western women choices that our mothers, much less our grandmothers, could never have imagined. My own mother left school at sixteen. Neither of my grandmothers ever even learnt to drive a car. None went to college.

Yes, women have made huge strides in a short span of human history. But the unexpected gift of so much choice is that we're now working overtime to catch up on so many measures, and so we feel like we're perpetually falling short. It's unsurprising that studies, such as one from Wharton Business School that tracked wellbeing over 35 years, found that women today rate themselves with lower levels of wellbeing than they did in the 1970s.

It seems that no matter how hard we try, we're still coming up short. That we're not accomplished *enough*. Not together *enough*. Not experienced *enough*. Not clever *enough*. Not worthy *enough*. Not capable *enough*. Not leaderlike *enough*. Not slim or sexy or stylish *enough*.

And even when we rush through our days like Tigger on Red Bull, trying to fit everything in, we can't shake a lingering sense of inadequacy.

If only we had more time.

If only we knew what we were doing.

If only we knew how to keep more balls in the air.

If only we had more confidence ... or were better with money, smarter with business, more comfortable with networking, less worried about (*fill in the blank*).

If only we could really trust in ourselves that, no matter what happens, we can handle it; that no matter what we accomplish — or don't — we'll be fine. Actually, better than fine; that we will be *enough*, regardless. Only then will we truly know that we are innately worthy, powerful beyond measure, and that nothing and no-one outside of us can take that power from us.

Unless we give it to them.

Which is why I'm truly pleased you've landed in this chapter. Because I wrote it for women just like you — brave-hearted women who want to live a meaningful life that lights them up but too often don't think they can.

The #metoo movement sent out a global rallying cry for women across the world to reclaim their power, to shed their shame, own their worth, use their voice and make a stand for genuine equity across gender and across humanity. I truly believe there has never been a better moment to be a woman. If #metoo held one overriding message, it was this: women will no longer quietly tolerate what they formerly thought they must.

Yet the rise of women doesn't require the fall of men. If history tells us anything it's that society doesn't benefit when we diminish one group to elevate another. This is not some zero-sum game that requires us to reduce, demean or disparage the 'other'. Rather, it's about becoming equal partners on a level field. As Melinda Gates wrote in *The Moment of Lift*, 'Male dominance is harmful to society because any dominance is harmful.' In business, politics, entertainment, athletics, education — when a culture of dominance is broken, it activates power in us all.

The ultimate goal is 'the rise of both women and men from a struggle for dominance to a state of partnership,' wrote Gates. Her sentiments were echoed by Nicholas Kristof and Sheryl WuDunn who wrote in *Half the Sky*: 'When women progress, we all progress. The greatest threat to extremism isn't drones firing missiles but girls reading books.'

As I've seen time and time again working in diverse organisations across the world, the best decisions are made and the best outcomes are achieved — economically, environmentally and socially — when teams harness the full value of diversity. Gender diversity ranks high among them.

Or course, this book is not about parity. It's about power. About *your* power. More so, what blocks you from exercising it fully.

Power — defined most simply as 'our ability to affect change' — has no gender. Nor does it reside only in those who win it in elections or were born into it. It resides within each of us. Yet our mental template of what power looks like is often male, and often in a business suit.

Regardless of how power-*full* or power-*less* you perceive yourself to be, consider for a moment that you may actually have more power than you have been conditioned to believe.

As Alice Walker wrote in *The Color Purple*, 'The most common way people give up their power is by thinking they don't have any.'

You would not be reading this now if you had no interest in living a more empowered life, a life in which you hold yourself in your power, rather than give your power away to other forces, whether they be your doubts, your boss, your partner or those whose approval you seek. So I hope that something you read here will embolden you to create a manifesto for your own life, empowering you to move beyond the cages of the roles and labels you've put on yourself.

THE JUGGLEHOOD ACT IS REAL. BUT CHANCES ARE, YOU CAN HANDLE MORE THAN YOU'VE GIVEN YOURSELF CREDIT FOR.

As I write now, I'm in the midst of doing my PhD (and regularly second-guessing the logic that had me sign up!) while parenting four kids over two continents — two now at college and two in their final two years of high school. I'm also supporting my husband as he pursues his calling to leadership in the corporate realm. Somewhere in between all that, I try to be a good (or just half decent) friend and sister and daughter and ambassador for an inclusive and equitable world I want to live in. I also travel frequently giving keynote speeches and facilitating leadership programs, as that's how I pay my kids' tuition. (Writing books has definitely not been a money spinner ... well, not yet, anyway!) So you might say I have a full plate. But then again, what woman doesn't feel that way? And if there's one thing I've learnt over the last two decades of juggling the responsibilities of *trying* to be a loving, playful and present mother while pursuing my own calling, it's that we women often underestimate ourselves and can be our own worst enemy.

Overcoming this sometimes requires us to say no to the good things we feel pressured to do so we can create space for the great things we'd love to do. Other times we need to lower the perfectionist bar we set for ourselves and embrace 'good enough is good enough'. This can apply to anything from our wardrobe to our waistline. And sometimes we have to be really honest about where our fear of social disapproval is calling the shots and holding us captive to social conventions so we can live life on *our* terms.

Not every woman aspires to climb to the ranks, build a business, write a book or raise kids (much less four!). All of which is perfectly okay. Just because some are inspired to run for public office or lead a multi-national corporation doesn't make your contribution any less valuable. What matters is that what you are doing is meaningful to you and you're not selling out on all that you could be and do for fear you don't have what it takes.

Too many women do.

EMPOWERING YOURSELF REQUIRES CHANGING HOW YOU THINK ABOUT POWER.

The 'Notorious RBG' — Supreme Court Justice Ruth Bader Ginsberg — once said 'Women belong in all places where decisions are being made.'

Why do so few women sit in the places where decisions are being made? One commonly cited explanation is the 'gender confidence gap'. It's a convenient explanation that blames women for where they sit relative to men on pay scales, promotion lists and leadership tables. Yet the hard truth is that many women aren't as confident as many men for good reasons — for thousands of years, the systems women have lived in have made it much harder (if not outright impossible) for them to rise and get ahead. This is not to blame men for the fact that the playing field has not been even. Rather, it is to state the obvious.

Men have faced fewer obstacles in everything from climbing the corporate ladder to running for public office to securing venture capital. And while the winds are changing, they still do.

But it's not just that. Gendered norms, expectations and biases are embedded into our thinking from the start. Even the most well-meaning parents can inadvertently instil double standards and tilted expectations into their sons and daughters. Without realising it, we often encourage boys to take risks (parents are more likely to help their sons up onto the monkey bars than their daughters, as though girls' bones are more fragile) and reward them for their strength and bravery (creating its own problems for men, as I'll get to in the next chapter). In the process, boys build a higher tolerance for risk and greater resilience for bouncing back when they've been knocked down.

By the age of six, girls are less likely to report they can be 'really really smart' compared to boys. By middle school, they're already opting towards 'pink collar' jobs. By high school, many girls have learnt that their biggest asset is their looks and their esteem rests heavily on people affirming as much. Little wonder so many young women measure their value from their social media feed. The more likes they get, the more worthy they feel. For today. Tomorrow, it begins all over.

We can rail against the insanity of it all. We can tell our daughters they are more than their Instagram following or Snapchat streaks. We can praise their intelligence and celebrate their accomplishments. But we are swimming upstream against the marketers and mass media. The fact that the media focuses far more on what human rights lawyer Amal Clooney wears than on the work she does is evidence of this.

Even girls who've been cocooned in a genderless education system and embark on their careers with confidence and ambition often exceeding that of their male counterparts eventually land in a workforce that was not designed for them. Once there, they discover, as Jamila Rizvi wrote in *Not Just Lucky*, that 'the ground is not tilted in their favour and, more often than not, is tilted against them'. They often also struggle to find female role models, to secure senior sponsors or to identify with a template for power. Likewise, when women act like women, they are evaluated as less leader-like — and when they act like men in ways that are incongruent with traditional feminine norms, they are penalised for not being feminine enough. It leaves many women in a Catch-22, damned if they do and damned if they don't. Yet just because it's always been this way doesn't mean it must always stay that way. Conforming to norms doesn't change them. We must actively work to shift the norms that have too long hemmed us in and undermined our self-belief.

WE CANNOT CHANGE THE NORMS THAT WORK AGAINST US IF WE'RE ALWAYS BENDING TO CONFORM TO THEM.

Studies show that within ten years of entering the workforce, many women dial down their ambition relative to their male peers. I was one of those data points. I started my career all guns blazing in the graduate program of an international corporation that provided excellent training and development opportunities. Yet when I had my first child (which lined up with moving countries for Andrew's job), I left an office behind, opting instead to do part-time consulting. At that point, with no role models in sight, I simply could not see another path forward. Were there other options? Of course. But at that juncture in my life, I couldn't see any that were palatable.

Andrew's career took the lead early on (despite the fact that we had been sitting on similar rungs on the corporate ladder when we met) and I didn't question it. It was just the way things were. And for the most part, it has worked. Yet without his support to begin a whole new career path, amid the chaos of our young family (which often left him with four kids to bath and wrangle to bed), I'm not sure I'd have ever dared to have done all that I have. His faith in me bolstered my own countless times.

One of the best pieces of advice I've come across for women who are navigating the conflicting demands of motherhood and career is by Jennifer

Martineau and Portia Mount, authors of *Kick Some Glass*, who wrote 'Don't drop out, power down.' That is, give yourself permission to 'lean out' at different points in your life. Just don't let fear of not having what it takes drive you to drop out all together.

My circumstances may be unique to me, yet they hold a lot in common with those of many other women. They also explain the 'leaky pipeline', the term coined to explain the drop-off of women in the management pipeline. As the next season of life with no children at home draws closer, I sometimes wonder where I may have ended up had I stayed within the corporate ranks. Yet I have no regrets. Forging my own 'path less travelled' meant less perks and less money for many years, but it gave me flexibility. And that, I've prized dearly.

It's also afforded me the privilege of working with thousands of women all around the world, from trailblazing entrepreneurs to corporate high-fliers to mothers with small home-based businesses and everything in between. As diverse as our paths may be, I've found common patterns of thought and behaviour that hold many of us women back. So to keep it simple here are my ten commandments of courage for women who want to roar, but who too often doubt if they can.

Ten Commandments of Courage For Brave-Hearted Women

1. Be nice, but not too nice.

As the big sister of seven I learnt to be bossy early. Yet let's face it, no-one likes being bossed around. That said, unless you're willing to speak up, push back, set boundaries and assert yourself when the need arises, you can end up feeling resentful as other people's priorities and desires take precedence over your own.

You can still be nice to people and let them know they need to lift their game. You can still be nice and decline an invitation. And you can still be agreeable and disagree with another's opinion or call someone out for poor behaviour.

So beware of over-applying the golden rule. Sometimes it's less about treating people as you'd like to be treated and more about teaching people how you'd like to be treated. So be nice, but stand your ground, set your boundaries and cower to no-one.

2. Embrace imperfection.

Sure, preparation can be useful. But too often women overprepare as a way of safeguarding against the chance of failure. If I'd waited to be a brilliant coach before I ever started coaching, I'd still be in training. If I'd waited until I could give a killer speech before I stepped onto a stage, I'd still be practising in front of the mirror. And as for writing a perfect book, well ... you would not be reading this!

Men are generally more comfortable with just diving in and figuring out how to fly the plane as they go. So we women have some catching up to do.

If this is something you're struggling with, please re-read chapter 3. Out loud!

3. Take the compliment!

When it comes to accepting praise, many women squirm. It's time to change that!

Christine Lagarde, President of the European Central Bank, was asked in an interview if she minds when people ask her for a selfie. 'Not at all,' she replied, going on to explain that she banks away the positive attention for the times when she's getting flak instead of flattery.

You are good at many things. Perhaps exceptionally good at a few. Own that fact. And when people compliment you on what you've done, accept it graciously. No deflecting, no brushing it off or talking yourself down or minimising it with, 'Oh it was nothing, I just got lucky.' Rather, just thank them with grace and gratitude. And let the truth they speak sink in, accumulating the emotional deposits for the day you need to draw on them! It will come.

4. Defy convention, express your difference.

Real liberation is about freedom of self-expression. Yet since women are communal by nature, we can easily become captive to the approval of the group. But here's the deal: when you're preoccupied with trying to fit in, you negate the very difference your difference makes. This isn't about being a non-conformist for the sake of it; rather, it's about recognising that when all you do is conform, all you offer is conformity. Owning your difference and expressing yourself authentically and unapologetically might sometimes raise eyebrows. So be it. They'll be the eyebrows of those held captive to social approval. Far better to be true to yourself than spend your life seeking the approval of others. To quote Dr Seuss, 'Be who you are, because those who mind don't matter and those who matter don't mind.' The best part: when you show up in the world as your own person, unbound by convention, you empower others to do the same. That's how real liberation is won.

5. Dare to ask.

When Simone Outteridge was promoted to a high-profile role, she didn't want anyone to think she couldn't handle the workload. 'So I worked my tail off and never asked for any support despite the enormity of the role. It nearly killed me, but a year later I got promoted to another role. But here's the kicker, the first thing the guy who replaced me did was ask for an assistant.' He got one soon after.

It's not just asking for help that many women are reticent about. It's asking for *anything*. Catherine Sandler, a leadership researcher, found that four out of five women find it 'extremely difficult' to express concerns and make clear and concise requests.

Of course this behaviour is adaptive in so far as it avoids the backlash women can face when they transgress on 'nice girls don't ask' norms. Many women I know, myself included, were admonished as girls for behaving in ways that might be perceived as self-serving. Don't be pushy or greedy or difficult. Just do a good job and don't complain. No-one likes a whinger.

It's true. No-one likes a constant complainer. Yet in our effort not to be seen as one, we can conflate making any request for ourselves with being demanding or difficult. In doing so, we reject ourselves long before anyone else has the chance.

At the heart of why many women don't ask for something to help them thrive and rise is the belief that they're unworthy of it. So if a thought remotely resembling 'Who am I to ask for that?' ever rumbles through your head, flip it on its head by asking: 'Who am I *not* to ask for that?'

Opportunities rarely go to the busiest worker bees, highest IQs or most selfless martyrs. They go to those who advocate for them. The fact that men tend to rate their value higher is not their fault. It just points to the importance of being extra vigilant in not allowing social conditioning to dictate the value we place on ourselves or how much (or little) we settle for. A study of MBA graduates at Carnegie Mellon found female students asked for, on average, a 30 per cent lower starting salary than their male peers.

So get clear on your ideal outcome, make your case, and make your ask. Not in an entitled way. Not in an aggressive way. Not in a resentful way. But in a direct way that conveys your belief in your value. Doing so affirms your own sense of worthiness for greater things ahead.

6. Save your 'sorry'.

I know I'm not the world's best writer and that I could be messing up how I say this and I appreciate there are people who know far more about this than me and I certainly don't want to step on anyone's toes, but I'm just wondering, and sorry if I'm getting this wrong, but maybe a few of us women could stop apologising for our opinion before we even speak it? Like I say, I'm far from an authority but maybe ...

Sent you to sleep yet? My point: apologising for your opinion dilutes its value. It also undermines the trust others place in you and the trust you place in yourself.

So stop apologising for your opinion to mitigate the risk of stepping on toes. Save your sorry for the time when you make a real mistake. Because while the paragraph above may have been a facetious way of making my point, the fact that studies find women tend to preface their opinion with some form of apology four times more often than men shows it's not entirely off the mark. Sorry not sorry.

7. Don't 'should' on yourself.

The word 'should' is just a word, yet it often reflects social expectations we feel pressured to comply with. It's why we can very easily find ourselves living 'shouldie' lives, making decisions that are guided far more by what others expect of us than what we truly want for ourselves.

When it comes to raising kids, 'shoulds' abound. You *should* breastfeed until twelve months. You *should* have them in swimming lessons by one, toilet-trained by two, bilingual by three, reading chapter books by four, at grade 3 violin by five ... and on it goes. It's my strong belief that it's far better for our children to have a happy parent than a perfect one. So, trust yourself and do what works for *you* and *your* family and don't let fear of social disapproval get you sucked into living your life according to what others think you should do.

YOU CANNOT BE A STAND FOR THOSE YOU LOVE IF YOU ARE NOT FIRST BEING A STAND FOR YOURSELF.

8. Amplify the sisterhood.

When President Obama took office in the White House, a third of the top aides he appointed were women. Yet despite the increased female representation, it wasn't long before many found themselves feeling talked over and sidelined from decision making, their input ignored or less valued than that of their male counterparts.

As the women of the West Wing began sharing their frustration with each other, they decided to adopt a strategy they called 'amplification'. Whenever one of their female colleagues would share an opinion on an important issue, the other women seated around the table would repeat it, attributing credit to their colleague for making such a salient point. By doing so, it helped raise their visibility and ensure their contribution was properly recognised. According to one female aide, Obama soon began to notice and started calling more often on the women in the room.

This anecdote supports studies that prove the real impact of women proactively championing other women. However, studies also show women tend to have smaller and less diverse networks than men. Which is why it's so important to proactively nurture a diversity of relationships and go out of your way to support the visibility of other women, including those with whom you might have less in common. As Australia's former Foreign Affairs Minister Julie Bishop said, 'Always back other women! They might be your competitors, but they are not your enemies.'

My many moves around the world have required re-establishing both social and professional networks multiple times. As I've relocated to new cities, countries and continents, women — from friends to distant acquaintances — have led the charge in connecting me into their social and professional networks, helping me feel part of a supportive community faster than I ever could have otherwise. As I've repeatedly experienced facilitating my women's retreat weekends, a special kind of magic occurs when big-hearted women come together to support each other.

9. Own your beauty, but don't let it own you.

We live in a world that worships 'body beautiful' and celebrates perfectionism even as it censures it. At every turn we are bombarded with airbrushed images of how a woman *'should'* look (assuming, that is, she wants to be loved). Self-doubt sells products; insecurity fuels sales. The beauty industry would require a total makeover if, God forbid, women ever started feeling totally secure in themselves.

Yet here's the deal: if you derive your self-worth from how you look, you'll spend your lifetime feeling insecure. It's taken me decades, but I've grown to love my soft curves (most days; some days I still regress). And I've come to know that who I am is not how I look and, more so, how I look can never, *never,* measure who I am. My body is perfectly imperfect, much like the rest of me!

My worth does not come from my outward appearance. It comes from my inner conviction to own it. The same is true for you!

If Michelle Obama defined herself by her ability to squeeze into a sample-size dress she would never have become one of the world's most admired women. It's the fact that she embraces her body and defines her own worth that makes her such a powerhouse and inspirational role model for the force of feminine leadership.

Nothing makes a woman more attractive than being grounded in her innate worthiness and at home with her body and innate beauty, neither preening it nor demeaning it. Just owning it.

So just for today, live as though you are every bit as worthy and wonderful as any woman you've ever admired. Then tomorrow, repeat. Then every day thereafter.

10. Say no to the good and yes to yourself!

How long since you've disappointed someone by saying no? Many women struggle to say no because, let's face it, saying yes is what others want to hear. Yet it's impossible for any busy woman (or man) to live a great life if their fear of not pleasing *everyone* keeps them from ever disappointing *anyone*.

Of course, there is nothing wrong with saying yes if it aligns with your priorities and values. But just be mindful, each time you say yes to anything you are, by default, saying no to whatever else you may have done with that time. Saying yes when your heart isn't in it often leads to resentment and frustration.

So next time you're feeling pressured to say yes to something that isn't lighting you up, tell them you'll get back to them tomorrow. It will buy you time to get clear about what matters most and summon your courage to respond with a very kind and gracious no. This is not about rejecting another person, it's about saying yes to yourself. Only by saying no to the good can you create space for the great.

* * *

Each time we own our unique brand of brilliance and beauty, and defy the norms that have hemmed us in, we elevate everyone around us. The more women unite to own their strength while embracing their femininity, the faster we elevate all humanity.

So yes, my dear fellow woman, you have everything it takes to roar loud and rise strong and make your mark.

Be the role model you wish you had in your formative years. Embody grace *and* grit. Embrace feminine *and* fierce. Lead with courage *and* compassion.

This world is hungry for women to claim their power and redefine it. As Beyoncé said, 'I don't like to gamble, but if there's one thing I'm willing to bet on, it's myself.'

Bet on yourself.

'Genuine vulnerability represents a form of power. When you risk vulnerability you'll find new depth in your relationships and new strength in yourself.'

Mark Manson

8

Dear Men

Your greatest strength is found in vulnerability

As the daughter of a good man, wife of a good man, friend to good men and mother of three fine young good men-in-the-making, I know there are very good men the world over.

I also know that men the world over face pressures today that their fathers and grandfathers never did; pressures that have challenged the trust they once placed in themselves.

In some ways, it's a challenging time to be a man. As women are finding their voice and claiming seats at the table, many men find themselves feeling increasingly displaced, devalued and disempowered. Some have confided to me how they even feel threatened and sidelined, as though they are being vilified for the crime of being born male. Others are simply confused, baffled about how best to express themselves or engage with women in the post #metoo world. Perhaps you are one of them.

So, if you're reading this now and have in any way felt as though you've been painted with the same broad brush used for Harvey Weinstein, I'm sorry. The fact that you've picked up this book tells me you sometimes wrestle with doubt and struggle to feel as sure of yourself as you'd like to be, and as some assume you should be. Perhaps you also sometimes feel like an imposter, waiting to be found out as not nearly as strong or smart or self-assured as people seem to believe. Maybe you've grown weary of feeling like you're supposed to have all the answers and fix all the problems of those around you. Or perhaps you just long to feel truly validated and worthy — seen for who you are rather than the 'role' others have cast you to play.

As I woman I'm mindful that I have no claim to know what it's like to be a man.

But men and women share the same innate hunger for belonging and meaning, and the equally instinctive fear of failure, rejection and irrelevance.

You want to be loved and feel respected — just like me. You want to feel connected and cared for — just like me. And you want to feel grounded in your innate worthiness and unafraid to face your challenges head on — just like me.

But not *just like me*. Just like *everyone*.

The challenge is that ever since you were born the world around you has been letting you know how a 'real man' should be. Strong. Stoic. Independent. Accomplished. In control. A study by Unilever found that most young men today still feel pushed to live within the confines of a 'Man Box' — a rigid construct of cultural ideas about the male identity that they found makes young men more likely to act with bravado to mask deep insecurities and less likely to seek help or express vulnerability. They identified core themes of how 'real men' should act. These included

- being self-reliant and self-sufficient — particularly in regard to their physical, mental and emotional health

- being strong and tough — ready to defend their reputation and show emotional invulnerability

- being physically attractive, hetero and hypersexual — unambiguously straight and eager for sexual conquest

- being controlling and complying to rigid gender norms, particularly around the division of domestic/caregiving workloads and being the provider (i.e. real men should be the ones to 'bring home the bacon' ... or at least more bacon than their female partners).

Chances are there have been many times you've felt pressure to 'man up'. Perhaps the pressure has made it hard for you to connect with, much less outwardly express, your deeper needs and emotions. After all, the childish playfulness and sensitivity of the boy you once were likely had no place in the world of the man you felt you had to become.

The term 'toxic masculinity' has arisen from the growing awareness of the harm that gender norms and expectations have inflicted on men (and, by default, on women), affecting their ability to forge healthy, emotionally intimate and rewarding relationships. Men are 32 per cent less likely to visit a doctor, and around the world men are three to four times more likely to die by their own hand than women, despite women experiencing higher rates of depression. The findings of the Unilever study were so strong, consistent and alarming that the economic costs of rigid masculine norms were estimated to cost to the tune of over twenty billion dollars a year to the US, UK and Mexican economies where the study was conducted.

FEAR OF APPEARING WEAK DISCONNECTS US FROM OUR TRUE STRENGTH. ONLY THROUGH EXPOSING THE TRUTH OF OUR LIVES CAN WE ACCESS OUR DEEPEST SOURCE OF POWER.

Of course there's nothing wrong with a man conforming to his gender norms, talking sports or stocks, or spending Saturday fixing the leaking tap or watching a game, if that's what he wants to do. Yet, too often, many men struggle to talk about what might be weighing on their hearts. Too uncomfortable, too vulnerable, too risky. With so much social pressure on men to appear 'strong', 'in control' and 'self-reliant', it's little wonder so many live with a 'feelings phobia', afraid to feel — much less to share — the true depth of the emotions swirling within. As Bryan Reeves wrote for The Good Men Project, 'We don't even tell our intimate partners our deepest truths.'

We human beings are emotional creatures. The more open we are to experiencing the full gamut of the emotional spectrum, the richer our experience of life. While it would be nice to hand pick the emotions we feel, when we try to numb or shut ourselves off from feeling emotions on one end of the spectrum, we also shut ourselves off from feeling emotions on the other. In doing so we constrict our emotional bandwidth for life itself, confining ourselves to a life only partially felt.

Ever eaten a delicious meal with a nasty ~~man~~ head cold and were unable to taste the full flavours, much less to savour them? Well, when you don't allow yourself to feel your most vulnerable feelings, you shut yourself off from savouring life's true sweetness and from experiencing your true strength. It also puts you at risk of working out the emotions you won't let yourself feel on the people around you. Often those you love most. The outcome only inflicts a wound on everyone's heart and a deeper wedge in the emotional distance between you.

ACTING STRONG IS STILL ACTING. THE FEAR THAT KEEPS YOU FROM OWNING YOUR VULNERABILITY ALWAYS ENDS UP BEING WORKED OUT ON THOSE AROUND YOU.

Braving vulnerability expands the full bandwidth of your humanity, providing a gateway to access your deepest strength. By allowing yourself to feel what you may not want to feel, it doesn't make you weaker. Rather it cracks you open to access a whole new level of courage, deepening the trust you have in yourself to meet life at its rawest edge in those moments when it can matter the most.

Vulnerability is also the gateway to true human connection, as I'll get to in chapter 10. As Robert Glover wrote in *No More Mr. Nice Guy*, 'Humans are attracted to each other's rough edges.'

No-one would dispute that removing our armour comes with a risk. Studies show that men who display sensitivity can face backlash similar to women who display assertiveness. A field study led by Ashleigh Rosette at Duke University found that when male (but not female) leaders ask for help, they are more at risk of being viewed as less competent, capable and confident. And when men make themselves vulnerable by disclosing a weakness at work, there is a higher chance of them being perceived to have lower status. Hand in hand with this is other research which finds that men who show sadness at work are more likely to be thought of as less deserving of that emotion than women.

This creates its own double bind for men — shamed for being 'too tough' when they keep their masculine armour intact; penalised for being 'too soft' when they violate masculine norms and lower their guard. It begs the question, is the risk of appearing weak and emotionally exposed worth it? I believe that it is. Exposing the truth of our lives to the world — our struggles, our setbacks, our deep-seated fears — is the ultimate risk. Yet it also holds the ultimate reward: releasing us from the fear that can hold our lives hostage.

WITHOUT RISKING BEING FULLY SEEN IN THE WORLD, YOU RUN THE GREATER RISK OF NEVER FEELING YOU FULLY BELONG IN THE WORLD.

Unless you're willing to risk being seen fully for who you are — complete with your toughest struggles and deepest fears — you run the ultimate risk of never feeling like you truly belong in the world at all. In doing so, you can inadvertently isolate yourself from those around you. On recounting his career as a professional athlete, NFL footballer Jimmy Stewart said how he would cry alone nearly every day, badly needing to talk to somebody but too afraid to open up and reveal his vulnerability. While CTE (brain injury) is often attributed to the high rates of depression and suicide among NFL players, he believes the cause goes much deeper. As he shared with *ESPN Magazine*, 'CTE can cause symptoms of depression, but it's isolation and invulnerability that causes you to commit suicide'.

In *The Road Less Travelled*, psychiatrist M. Scott Peck wrote that 'There can be no vulnerability without risk; there can be no community without vulnerability; there can be no peace, and ultimately no life, without community.' Yes, men are wired to hunt together, work together and laugh together, but they are also meant to cry together and heal together. No-one is meant to bear the burden of their inner lives alone. It brings to mind a fable I once heard that speaks to the importance of opening ourselves up to those around us, despite the risk we take from lowering our guard.

It was an exceptionally cold winter and many animals died from exposure to the bitter chill. The porcupines, realising the situation, decided to group together to keep warm. While this covered and protected them, the quills of each porcupine also wounded their closest companions.

After a while, they decided to distance themselves one from the other. Yet before too long, they began to die, one after another, alone and frozen. Realising the situation, they had to make a choice — to accept the wounds from the quills of their companions or to disappear entirely. Wisely, they decided that the risk of being vulnerable to the wounds was less than the risks of isolation. Sometimes the wounds of their companions stung deeply, but they learnt to live with them. The alternative was not living at all.

You may want to go it alone, but revealing your fears allows them to dissipate whereas masking them cements them into your being. It's by embracing vulnerability that you can access your greatest strength and build the bonds — with both men and women — that allow you to grow even stronger.

THE MASKS WE WEAR TO PROTECT US CAN MAKE US A STRANGER TO OURSELVES AND TO OTHERS.

Many men have been shamed from a young age for showing anything that remotely resembled weakness or betrayed the masculine norm. *Don't be a girl. Man up. Toughen up. Stop being a sissy ... a wimp ... a crybaby.* Equally toxic is parents justifying their son's disrespectful behaviour with comments like 'Boys will be boys.' Sure, boys will be boys, and boys will act boisterously (I know, I have rowdy sons, now all over six feet tall, still wrestling each other), but an abundance of testosterone is no excuse for a lack of respectfulness.

Living in a culture that has normalised 'only girls cry' has exacted a profound collective toll. Not only can it leave men moving through life cut off from those around them at an emotionally intimate level, but it also leaves them disconnected from the deepest part of themselves. The part which, when the heat turns up in life, provides their greatest source of strength, resilience and, in the wake of trauma, what is called 'post traumatic growth'.

So it is that often the 'worst thing that ever happened' to a man, often in his middle years, can ultimately turn into the 'best thing that ever happened' (albeit a profoundly painful crucible at the time). It is the day when, to paraphrase Anaïs Nin, that you discover that the risk of remaining tight inside the armour grows greater than the risk of taking it off.

THE 'WORST THING THAT EVER HAPPENED' HOLDS THE SEED TO BECOME 'THE BEST THING THAT EVER HAPPENED'.

In his book *Manhood*, Steve Biddulph refers to this crucible experience as the 'Time of the Ashes'. It can come in many forms. The loss of a child in miscarriage, or one born with a disability. A business that goes under, or a life's savings lost. Retrenchment. Addiction. Infidelity. Illness. Injury. Death of a friend. Ambition crushed. Reputation ruined.

At the heart of life's crucible experiences is the shattering of our identity into a thousand pieces; the loss of the person we'd told ourselves we were. Strong. Invincible. Immune to the struggles of others.

As Biddulph wrote, 'You do not have to experience total devastation in order to grow into a mature man, but it helps.' Yes, it helps to discover that you cannot get through this life in any way that's deeply meaningful if you're unwilling to lower your guard, to lean on others and let them in. 'Every man needs an ashes time in his life, to discover that, in spite of all optimism and effort, one is still vulnerable,' writes Biddulph.

> *If he can make the impressive and redemptive leap, if he doesn't snap shut the armour but stays open to the scorching bath of shame, the experience will change him, will wash away the dross and the pretence.*

It was a crucible experience for Kai-Fu Lee, a pioneer in artificial intelligence at Google, Microsoft, Apple and other companies, that sent him on a pilgrimage from head to heart. A self-confessed AI-obsessed workaholic who prioritised his work ethic over his family, a diagnosis of stage-four lymphoma was the catalyst required for Lee to confront his own mortality. 'That crisis brought me to a very dark place,' he wrote in *AI Superpowers*, 'one that challenged my deepest-held assumptions about what matters in life.'

Up until that point, Lee had engaged with the world as an algorithm needing to be solved. He approached every meeting in a detached mechanistic way, focused on how he could optimise each interaction for optimal outcomes. And then, at age fifty-two, he was told he may have just months to live. Unable to find an algorithm for this problem, he had no choice but to reassess how he had been living his life. 'I came to see how foolish it was to base my self-worth entirely on my accomplishments at work,' Lee wrote.

In the midst of confronting his death he realised that he'd neglected the most important part of life — the human capacity for compassion, connection and creativity. His cancer journey woke him up to life, shifted his priorities and helped him reframe AI through a far more holistic and human lens. AI may replace many jobs, but not those that require a capacity to love, connect and create. In his words, 'As AI will liberate us from routine work, it will free us to become more human, not less.'

EXPERIENCING THE FULLNESS OF OUR OWN HUMANITY REQUIRES THE COURAGE TO RISE ABOVE THE FEARS THAT MIGHT OTHERWISE HOLD US HOSTAGE.

Lee's crucible experience was the catalyst for his transformation from a high-achieving man to a deeply loving man. While his insights come from a unique vantage point, they hold a universal truth. Our freedom to become more human, not less, requires the courage to rise above the fears that might otherwise hold us hostage. True freedom can only ever be born by the death of the false self — the self that is founded in fear and fuelled by ego. So, to you, someone who craves true freedom (because what man doesn't?), might it be time to unshackle the chains that have kept your emotions at bay and isolated you from the hearts of those around you?

Of course, freedom comes in many forms. And one form is the freedom to live a life that aligns with the truth of who you are, not who others think you *should* be. It took a crucible experience for my friend (and fellow Aussie/American) Warwick Fairfax to discover this for himself. One that came in the cost of losing the very thing he had felt he'd been born to build: his family's 150-year-old media empire.

From the moment of his birth in Sydney, Australia, Warwick had been groomed to one day take over Fairfax Media, which was, at the time, one of

Australia's largest media companies, owning the country's leading papers (think the equivalent of *The Washington Post, The Wall Street Journal* and *The New York Times*). Growing up with extreme privilege, with Liberace performing in his lounge room, attending Oxford and then Harvard for his MBA, Warwick never questioned the idea that he was, indeed, born to build on his family's rich legacy. Soon after his father died in 1987, Warwick launched a multibillion-dollar takeover of the family company, to retain family control and change management. Yet by the time Warwick was 30, three years later, the family business had been lost under his watch and he had become the mockery of Australia's media, ridiculed for what they saw as his foolish decisions.

In the years that followed, Warwick slowly picked up the pieces of his shattered identity. As he did, he came to realise that in never questioning the vision his parents had for him, he had ventured down a path that was not only poorly aligned with his strengths but that he'd never considered the vision he truly wanted for himself. He discovered that there was a more worthy life's pursuit than success: significance. 'I grew up with about as much wealth and status as you could, but at the end of the day money doesn't satisfy,' Warwick told me. 'Significance is about serving a higher purpose, making the world a better place, helping others. Abundance is more than money. It's abundance in family and relationships.' (My podcast with Warwick, now a leadership coach and consultant, in which he recounts this crucible experience is worth a listen.)

> OPENING OUR HEARTS WIDE TO THE FULL
> SPECTRUM OF HUMAN EMOTION IS THE
> ULTIMATE ACT OF HEROISM.

A bird doesn't have to prove it can fly; it just flies. Likewise, a strong man doesn't have to prove he is strong, he's just strong. He doesn't have to flex his muscles, act with bravado, drive fast, out-drink his mates or get a woman into bed to prove his strength and masculinity. Only a truly strong man will own his failings, acknowledge his fear, admit he doesn't have all the answers and be willing to ask for help (or, when lost, for directions!).

And so, as counterintuitive as it may sound, it's by giving up trying to act strong that you open the gateway to access your greatest strength. It's okay to shed the 'strong man' armour, to ask for help, share your struggle and open your heart to the full spectrum of human emotions. After all, no feeling is final.

I've seen the power of vulnerability many times, both in programs I've led myself and others that I've attended. During one retreat I partnered with a man I'll call Tom. For several minutes we had to look at each other and take turns finishing the sentence 'I am ...' Having built rapport with Tom in the preceding days, I decided to reach out and hold his hands and, looking into his eyes, I sent him as much love as I possibly could. As tears welled in his eyes Tom shared, 'I am lovable.' I squeezed his hands tight, smiling. 'You are,' I said, 'You are very lovable.' And there we just sat, tears now streaming down his face, and mine, as he connected to the truth of his life and the wound of his childhood with a father too uncomfortable with his own vulnerability to express affection. Tom was lovable. He always had been. He'd just never truly felt it. Until then. It was beautiful. It makes me teary now just recalling the moment.

REAL COURAGE ARISES BY CONFRONTING OUR DEEPEST FEARS, NOT BY DENYING THEM.

If anything you're reading sounds a little soft or soppy or sentimental, just notice what part of you is reacting to it that way. What fear of vulnerability might lie beneath that? I'm not saying it is. I just invite you to consider it.

So many people grow up without affirmation of their innate lovability and without learning how to express deep love themselves. So if there's any part of you that has ever felt unlovable, let me just say this now from my heart to yours — you are lovable. No ifs and buts, no conditions or exceptions. Just deeply, innately deserving of love.

Hand in hand with being wholly lovable, you also have the capacity to be sensitive *and* strong, uncertain *and* assured, vulnerable *and* powerful ... *all at the same time.*

While you may already intellectually know this to be true, sometimes our 'emotional self' needs a little reminder. Years of conditioning can forge a deep imprint. Just as women can wrongly equate their worth with their looks, men can equate their self-worth with their net worth. Or, if not the money they've made, then the mountains they've climbed or the competitions they've won or the deals they've done. Yet who you are is innately lovable and wholly worthy, irrespective of any number, title, label or other measure on a socially constructed, superficially calibrated yardstick.

So if you are currently facing a situation in which you feel unsure, in which your doubts are ratcheting up and you're tempted to pull up your emotional drawbridge, stop for a moment. Retreat instead to somewhere quiet. Take a few minutes to breathe. Deeply. Observe the sensations swirling within you, however uncomfortable. Identify them by name: vulnerability, humiliation, shame, inferiority, fury, fear. Acknowledge them. Sit with them. Say 'yes' and invite them to reveal whatever lesson they have to teach you. Let them move through you as a cloud across the sky. Hold them gently, with compassion. Thank them for the gift they hold — for connecting you to your full humanity, in all its wonder and glory and messiness and imperfection and vulnerability.

WHAT IF YOU NEVER AGAIN HAD TO PROVE YOU WERE STRONG OR FEARED APPEARING WEAK?

This is, of course, true for all of us. But if you've been struggling with a challenge, feeling pressured to resolve it, to control it, to get it sorted in lightning speed, then it's all the more important to give yourself permission to lay your 'fix it' tools to the side for now, and just be with 'what is'. Permitting yourself to sit with 'what is', allowing your emotions to just be, will help you to realise that some things don't need fixing and others can't be fixed anyway. Which can come as a bit of a shock to men who've spent much of their adult lives in 'fix it' mode. I know this, because I married one. (Though he's in the reform phase now).

When we fully embrace the unique blueprint of who we are, we complement each other and become a greater conduit for good. It's in our diversity we can harness our greatest strengths. Of this I'm sure. When you truly own who you are (and accept who you're not), letting go of the need to prove or impress, to fix or force, you open the door to a deepened experience of life and a heightened appreciation of yourself.

So whatever you're facing, just know that you are already enough — you have nothing to prove and nothing to fix (including yourself). More so, that when you take away the pressure of trying to be someone more or stronger or bigger or better, you unlock the cage you've been living in, liberating yourself to grow into the magnificence of the whole-hearted person you were born to become.

BY GIVING UP TRYING TO PROVE YOU ARE BIGGER, BRAVER OR BETTER, YOU UNLOCK THE CAGE YOU'VE BEEN LIVING IN.

Our wounds hold the key to our awakening. When we avoid the pain of our wounds, we deprive ourselves of the freedom we might otherwise get from feeling them. As Rumi counselled, 'Don't turn away. Keep your gaze on the bandaged place, that's where the light enters.'

Start by reaching out to someone you trust and sharing what's going on for you. What's *really* going on. It will feel uncomfortable. Acutely so. Vulnerability always does. But embrace that feeling and don't let your fear of appearing weak keep you from accessing your greatest source of strength. The strength that comes from owning all of who you are, from leaning into those who love you, and from allowing yourself to connect at the most real and raw and heartfelt level. Nothing to hide, only to reveal.

'Vulnerability sounds like truth and feels like courage,' says Brené Brown. 'Truth and courage aren't always comfortable, but they're never weakness.'

Chances are you're more muscular than me, capable of lifting weights that I never will. Our emotional muscles are not all so different from our physical ones. If you haven't shared authentically for a while, it will leave you feeling very exposed. Yet the more you practise feeling your emotions, particularly those big uncomfortable ones you've likely spent years avoiding, the better you'll get at it. Over time, those emotions that were so awkward to feel, and so hard to express, will become less so. And as they do, it will open the door to a whole new realm of richness in your experience of life — a deeper capacity for joy, and intimacy, and connection, and compassion. Dare I say, by lowering your armour and untangling your heart from old notions of strength, you will transform your very experience of being alive.

'The best and most beautiful things in this world cannot be seen or even touched. They must be felt with the heart,' wrote Helen Keller.

Trust more in your heart, not just your head.

You've got this.

the
becoming

'Faith is to believe what you do not see; the reward of this faith is to see what you believe.'

St Augustine

9
Choose Faith Over Fear
A greater force has your back

'Live life as if everything is rigged in your favour,' wrote the Sufi mystic Rumi over eight hundred years ago. Yet let's get real here — living your life as though the universe has your back takes some major audacity. The audacity to place your trust in some higher force that cannot be seen; to believe in a power that cannot be proved.

I'm mindful that the very word 'faith', and even more so the term 'spirituality', can trigger defensiveness for some. Having grown up in Australia's secular culture, I am aware of how quickly people can roll their eyes at the first whiff of anything remotely religious. So before I go on let me just clarify that this chapter is not about religion. While religion can provide a pathway to spirituality, it can also, as Sister Joan Chittister wrote, 'leave people in danger of being a keeper of the law rather than a seeker of truth.'

So this chapter is for 'seekers of truth'. It's about strengthening your connection to a deeper dimension of your own humanity; to a source of power that cannot be seen with the senses or measured with science. But then again, to paraphrase one of history's greatest scientists, Albert Einstein, not everything that can be measured matters, and not everything that matters can be measured. In fact Einstein once observed that,

> *When you examine the lives of the most influential people who have ever walked among us, you discover one thread that winds through them all. They have been aligned first with their spiritual nature and only then with their physical selves.*

Wrestling with the roots of who we are as human beings is a universal part of the shared human quest for growth; one that often leaves us with more questions than answers, learning how to make peace with the unknown and unknowable. Yet as the great management theorist W. Edward Deming once wrote, 'The most important things are unknown or unknowable.'

I believe there is a larger unknowable force at work in our lives. More so, that our ability to trust in ourselves — particularly when times are tough and fears loom large — often requires leaning into a source of power that transcends our intellectual faculties. I like to frame this force the same way French philosopher Pierre Teilhard de Chardin did when he wrote that we are not so much physical beings who have the occasional spiritual experience but rather we are 'spiritual beings having a physical experience'.

Spirituality is therefore not some 'new age' trend that entails burning incense sticks, wearing prayer beads and greeting everyone with 'Namaste'. Nor is it about going to church or daily Bible readings. Rather it is about opening ourselves up to connect with something that is greater than ourselves. The name you give it is entirely up to you. But as Dr John Swinton from the University of Aberdeen says,

> *Spirituality is the outward expression of the inner workings of the human spirit; an aspect of human existence that gives it its 'humanness' and helps us deal with the vicissitudes of existence.*

It encompasses the deep human yearning for meaning, purpose, love, authentic relationships and (for many), to quote Swinton, 'a sense of the Holy amongst us'.

FAITH DOESN'T REMOVE YOUR CHALLENGES;
IT TRANSFORMS YOUR RELATIONSHIP TO THEM,
ENABLING YOU TO EXPERIENCE THEM ALL THE
WAY THROUGH AND EMERGE FROM THEM
ALL THE MORE WHOLE.

Over the ages, spirituality has been conceptualised in many ways. The 12-Step Program of Alcoholics Anonymous uses the term 'Higher Power' to avoid alienating those whose notions of God are mired in exclusion or judgement. Of course, the name we give 'the Holy amongst us' matters far less than whether we are willing to risk faith in its existence. Which is why faith is, in and of itself, an act of courage. Because it requires us to take a risk. To risk that we could be wrong and that there may, in fact, be no higher or holier force at play that is orchestrating a divine plan for our life or anyone else's. However, having weighed up the options — to choose the path of faith or the path of fear — I see it as a risk that must be run.

Faith is deeply personal. So I have no desire to push my spiritual belief system on you (and I know it would be futile to try). My intention is solely to support you in deepening your own faith — in yourself and in an intelligence that transcends your own.

Before I continue, let me just say, 'choosing faith over fear' doesn't remove your challenges. Rather it transforms your relationship to them. A growing body of research has validated the connection between spirituality and wellbeing. One meta study by the Mental Health Foundation in the UK found spirituality can make a positive impact on mental health, wellbeing and recovery from mental illness. One study of women recovering from trauma identified spirituality as one of the four pillars that encouraged post-traumatic growth (the others being social connection, self-awareness, and a sense of purpose and meaning).

Likewise, certain elements of spirituality have been found to positively affect our physical health. One study by psychologists Kevin Seybold and Peter Hill found that emotions encouraged in many spiritual practices and religious traditions — such as hope, contentment, love and forgiveness — can positively affect neural pathways that connect to the endocrine and immune systems. These same traditions also tend to discourage negative emotions (such as anger and fear) that trigger the release of the neurotransmitter norepinephrine and of the endocrine hormone cortisol which, sustained over longer periods, inhibit the immune system, increasing the risk of infection, high blood pressure, stroke and cardiovascular disease.

You might say that in today's pressure-laden workplaces and world, where millions suffer unhealthy levels of stress, faith helps to reduce it. And in doing so, it can help ward off many of the ailments stress can cause (it's estimated that 90 per cent of doctor's visits are for stress-related ailments and complaints). In fact, there's a strong case to be made that faith has a significant medicinal value.

For 35 years, Dr George Vaillant directed the famous Harvard Study, the world's longest ever longitudinal study that has tracked the lives of 724 men, beginning with 268 Harvard sophomores in 1938. In his book *Spiritual Evolution*, Vaillant laid out a compelling scientific case for spirituality as a positive force in human evolution and longevity. He found that the positive emotions of love, hope, joy, forgiveness and compassion (located in a different part of the brain than dogmatic religious beliefs) are what allow us to thrive; to experience a deeper dimension of our own humanity and connect more deeply to the humanity in others. These emotions help us to 'broaden and build' — to thrive amid life's many challenges, widening our attention (literally, in that our peripheral vision is actually broadened!) and expanding our horizon of possibilities for action.

FAITH EXPANDS OUR BANDWIDTH FOR SEEING THE GOOD AND MAKING THE BEST OF DIFFICULT SITUATIONS.

On the flip side, operating without any spiritual belief system can make it more difficult to process our experiences through a larger lens and to draw positive meaning and purpose from them. Without any way to disrupt this heavier emotional state, it puts us at greater risk of being swallowed up by negative emotions — such as fear, anxiety, anger, despair and resentment. While all emotions can serve us, when we're unable to shift out of a negative emotional state it can stifle our natural creativity, confine what we see as possible, and keep us from seeing 'the forest for the trees' as we navigate our way forward.

Indian philosopher Shrii Shrii Anandamurti wrote that 'the force that guides the stars guides you too'. Faith in this force has sustained me during difficult times and helped me endure my heartaches with more grace than I would have otherwise. That's not to say I haven't felt anxiety, despair, grief or anger numerous times over the years. Rather, my faith that something good can be found, even amid the worst, has kept me from being lost to them.

One way to think of faith is through the lens of lightness and darkness. Light is not something you see, but rather it works to dissolve the dark, allowing you to see everything that might otherwise have been hidden. It's interesting that in the very first book of the ancient scriptures that made up the Old Testament, the first thing God did was to create light. Now, I'm no theologian, but I believe that faith creates a channel to connect to the light *within* you. And that by doing so, it enables you to see everything else more clearly, in a new light, and to trust yourself in a whole new — 'holier' — way.

WE ALL HAVE A LIGHT WITHIN US. FAITH ALLOWS US TO TURN UP THE BURNER WHEN WE FEEL DARKNESS PRESSING IN AROUND US.

My own spiritual belief system has been forged through the fires of my life, evolving most from the times when I've wrangled with painful realities and wrestled with the big gnarly questions. *Why this? Why me? Why now?* Having faith in something beyond my own intelligence has provided a deep well of courage, grace, hope and healing that's sustained me when I've felt myself being pulled down by the turmoil around me.

The decade that led up to the death of my youngest brother, Peter (the second youngest of the seven kids in my family) was one of these periods. Countless nights I lay awake trying to make sense of the senseless, fighting off anguish and despair, feeling confused and sad — sad for Peter, and sad for my parents, whose hearts were also torn as they leant deeply into their own faith to ward off despair.

Right through his twenties, Peter struggled to ward off the delusions and demons of schizophrenia. 'God, how can that be part of your plan?' I'd rail.

Witnessing someone I loved so dearly, a vibrant young man brimming with dreams and potential, slowly retreat into a dark prison of paranoia and despair was utterly heart-wrenching. As the years wore on, and it became harder to keep track of his admissions into psychiatric wards, my parents and other siblings struggled to hold on to hope for his recovery. As his visits to mental wards grew more frequent, and his relapses more severe, we each gradually downgraded own our best expectations and grieved the loss of the life Peter would never live.

When Peter took his life, on Easter Good Friday, 2011, our hearts were torn open. We grieved the memories that we would never get to make with Peter, the man he would never become, the mark he would never make. Our lives would go on, our bodies would age, but Peter's never would. He'd lived 31 years, yet, for the previous ten, he'd endured more torment and suffering than the rest of us had ever known. We didn't wonder why he took his life. As his demons grew louder and his delusions darker, Peter slowly lost all hope for a future devoid of acute anguish, shame and despair.

What good can come of this?

I journaled on this question many times in the years leading up to Peter's death and then even more fiercely in the months following it. It felt so cruel, so unjust, so wretchedly unfair. Peter was the star athlete in our family, my quick-witted little brother whose ability to spin a basketball on the end of his finger mesmerised my kids, particularly my oldest son Lachlan who looked up to his uncle Pete with a child's awe. Pete was cool, collected, funny … even the girls in my sister Anne's class in high school (one grade above him) had had crushes on Pete.

And yet his life had ended early. Too early. Tragically. In complete despair.

What good can come of this?

I sat with that question and allowed my tears to flow many times.

What good can come of this?

There was no happy ending to this story. No 'Well, it all worked out for the best' platitude could be applied.

What good can come of this?

'Well … maybe I can make some good from this,' I journaled one day. 'Maybe by allowing the sadness of his death to become a precious part of my own story, I can channel that grief into living a more meaningful, whole-hearted life myself. Maybe, amid my own heartache, I can find a place of peace and a deeper compassion for every person who has ever wondered "Why this? Why me? Why now?"'

Ah, so many good things can come from the most difficult.

A deep knowing that life is innately good, even when it's hard.

A faith that somehow, amid the ashes of the life we thought we would live, something of good can be resurrected.

A belief that no matter how unfair life can feel, or how unjust things may seem, we have within us the capacity to take what is left behind to build something better than we would have otherwise been able to do.

A newfound sense of ourselves ... of our innate strength to weather even the most brutal of storms and to emerge from them better off: more whole, more loving, more of whoever we were put on this earth to become.

A sense of connectedness, that our own small separate life is connected to a larger life force that can guide us far better than our intellect alone can ever do.

DON'T FORCE THE DOTS TO CONNECT.
RATHER, KEEP FAITH THAT YOU WILL ONE DAY
LIVE INTO THE ANSWERS.

Faith in some higher plan expands the light that can flow into our lives, helping us to see goodness in the midst of dark times. Even if only in glimpses. My own faith has not only buoyed me through my darker hours; it has expanded my bandwidth to see the goodness in others and to respond with compassion rather than judgement, hope rather than pessimism, and courage rather than fear. It lies at the foundation of everything I do, despite how fragile it can sometimes be. As Christian pastor Joel Osteen once said, on recounting how his father, who'd spent his life in the ministry, even at the end of his life struggled with the big questions of his faith: 'Doubt and faith can co-exist.' Oh, don't I know it!

My friend Kate believed that faith in a higher power was only for the weak: for those not strong enough to rely on their own intelligence. I met Kate in Port Moresby, Papua New Guinea, not long after I'd moved there. Kate was one of the most intelligent people I ever met. Quick-witted, fast on her feet, a speed reader and high achiever if ever I met one, Kate was one of the youngest people (and definitely one of the youngest women) to become partner at her esteemed law firm. Yet Kate also suffered from a deep sense of unlovability that stemmed from an unaffectionate father (whom I can only assume had been raised with a lack of love himself). I loved Kate.

For a couple of years, every weekday at noon, we'd head to the Aviat Club in Port Moresby to swim laps. Afterward, we'd sit beside the pool where we'd plan our expeditions to various remote corners of PNG and wax lyrical as we solved the problems of the world and, in particular, of PNG (which, at that time, was considered one of the most dangerous countries in the world outside a war zone, with endemic government corruption). We became close friends very fast, as you do in places where you live behind high barbed-wire fences patrolled by security guards and hear gunshots on a regular basis.

Kate introduced me to many philosophers and 'self-help' authors who later inspired my career change from marketing to coaching. Kate had read all their books. Knew all their theories. Could recite Rumi's verses, quote the mystics and 'success' gurus. But she flat out refused to have faith in something unverifiable: to believe that there was anything more to life than what one could experience or confirm directly with the senses. Her struggle with depression deepened after returning to Melbourne. Nothing those who loved her could do would ever be enough to mend the primal wound on her heart. And then one morning, shortly after a man she had hoped would love her pulled back, unready for a deeper commitment, she went out for a run and hanged herself under a tree.

I can never know how life might have unfolded differently for Kate had she opened her sharp mind and huge heart to the possibility of a source of intelligence greater than her own. If, in her final days, she'd been able to lean into faith of some kind, *any* kind — faith in her innate lovability, faith that the darkness she felt would eventually pass, or even faith that she could channel her pain into something that infused her life with a deeper sense of purpose. The darkness of despair overtook her, and ultimately cost Kate her life, robbing the world of her brilliance and taking from me an extraordinary human being whom I dearly loved. Whom many loved. That was nearly twenty years ago. I miss her still.

LEANING INTO FAITH WON'T DISSOLVE ALL CONCERNS AND WORRY, BUT IT WILL HELP YOU RISE ABOVE THEM WITH COURAGE AND WONDER.

In the end, all faith is an experiment. But as with any experiment, we cannot reap its fruit without first doing the experiment. It is not a marker of weakness; it's a marker of courage.

And so I choose faith. I figure it's better to risk believing in something that isn't — particularly when it so profoundly expands my capacity to thrive amid life's challenges — than to disbelieve in something that is. Not only does my faith make me a better and braver human being, it helps me show up in the world in ways that help others to put their bravest foot forward when they might otherwise be overtaken by fear. (I would never have dared to write this book if it didn't.)

Which is ultimately what this book is all about. Choosing faith over fear, putting your bravest foot forward and trusting that 'you've got this' even when you're not sure of what step to take after the one immediately ahead of you.

Right now, as I write these words, I have no clear path ahead. Andrew and I are working towards getting our family all on one continent, but the requisite visas and jobs and numerous other barriers still line the path before us. In fact, I'm not even certain which continent I'll be planted in by the time this book comes out (which is unsettling for my publisher as well as for me!). So while I'd much rather be just dishing out advice, I'm well and truly having to walk my own talk as I choose faith over fear. So here I am, writing the book I feel called to write, despite the less than ideal circumstances I find myself in. Might I one day regret not having held off until I'd had greater certainty before bringing this book into the world? Potentially. But choosing faith over fear also means choosing to take action amid the unknowing and not waiting for perfect conditions before stepping forward toward whatever pulls on your heart.

And on the days when my heart feels extra heavy and my mind is racing, I have to embrace my own humanity and lean into my faith that everything will eventually work out for the highest good.

I have that same faith for you also.

Faith it *until* you make it.

Faith guarantees nothing and yet it changes everything. So stumble as I may, each day I do my best to choose to show up as though everything is working out, even when I have no idea how. Choosing to live from faith helps me feel stronger, stand taller and speak new possibilities into life. On the flipside, living from fear does just the opposite. It leaves my nails shorter, my world smaller, my stomach knotted, and my heart constricted. Little wonder those who fall into anxiety end up sick.

The same is true for all of us. Focusing on what scares us only weakens our resolve, dims our light and dials up all the negative emotions that keep us from taking the very brave actions that would serve our highest good in those moments when courage matters most.

> *Your small self says: 'Once everything falls into place, then I'll have faith.'*
>
> *Your true self says: 'Have faith, and then everything will fall into place.'*

Time and time again, I've witnessed magical possibilities open up in people's lives when they consciously decide to walk the path of faith over fear, trusting in some higher order to what seems like total disarray. So if your cynicism is still running on high and your faith is fragile, I invite you to try a fun little experiment with yourself. Ask yourself this question:

> *What would you do right now if you had faith that everything will work out for your highest good (even if you've no clue how)?*

Whatever answer popped into your head, take a step in that direction. If it helped you stand any taller, breathe a little easier or act a little braver, perhaps it's worth trying again tomorrow.

Sure, there's a risk that you're just kidding yourself. Sure, your situation may get messier or muddier before it gets better. And sure, it may be that things will not work out just as you'd like them to. As Tal Ben-Shahar — whose course on happiness at Harvard University was the most popular in the university's history — shared with me, things don't always work out the way you think is best, but you can always make the best of how things work out.

So take the risk, embrace the mess, and dare to step forward amid all your uncertainty with faith.

'You can't connect the dots looking forward; you can only connect them looking backwards,' wrote Steve Jobs,

> *So you have to trust that the dots will somehow connect in your future. You have to trust in something — your gut, destiny, life, karma, whatever. This approach has never let me down, and it has made all the difference in my life.*

Just cast your mind back over the many challenging moments you've had in your life. I'm sure you can think of many times you wondered and worried if you'd be able to handle what was coming your way. A bankruptcy, new baby, dying parent, broken marriage, messy law suit ... some unexpected and unplanned challenge you felt ill-equipped to handle.

Yet you did.

Sure, you had to be braver than you wanted to be. But you stepped up and you handled it and you figured it out. In the process, you grew stronger and cultivated gifts you might not have otherwise known you had. In fact, you wouldn't be who you are today had you not had that experience, as difficult or painful as it may have been.

So too, one day you will look back on where you are now and all the dots will connect in ways that are impossible to see from your current vantage point. When they do, you will realise how everything you experienced was part of what was required for you to grow into the person you eventually became and to make the mark on the world that you eventually made. You would never have experienced this fullness of life had everything gone just as you wanted.

EVEN THE GNARLIEST PROBLEMS HAVE A WAY OF WORKING OUT IN THE END. SO IF THEY HAVEN'T WORKED OUT YET, IT'S BECAUSE YOU'RE NOT AT THE END.

So whatever you are dealing with now, trust that the dots will eventually connect. And when fear rises up, keep faith.

Keep faith that if you feel a tug on your heartstrings, it's there for a reason.

Keep faith that if you take that leap, you'll not fall when you land.

Keep faith that your current situation holds a lesson to serve your highest good.

Keep faith that however dark your days, the light will again shine through.

Most of all, keep faith that the spirit within you is strong enough to meet any challenge and rise to any moment.

So focus just on this moment before you right now and release your worries about those ahead. After all, given our mind's tendency to 'catastrophise', your darkest fears are the least likely to eventuate.

Faith is a muscle that grows stronger with practice. By choosing faith over fear, particularly on the days when fear looms largest, you will gradually arrive at the moment Albert Camus described so beautifully — that 'in the midst of winter, I finally learned that there was in me an invincible summer'.

If your analytical brain is still screaming 'Hogwash!', then just try doing a little experiment and ask that invisible, unproven, unverifiable, inexplicable force if it would give you some sign in the days ahead.

Then pay attention. *Close attention.*

You live in the universe and the universe lives in you. It conspires for your highest good, but you must do your part.

Choose faith over fear. And, in the darkness of mid-winter, keep faith, press on and trust that within you lays an invincible summer.

And on those particularly testing days, when you're most tempted to curl up in a ball and surrender to despair, I've found that the most important thing is to remember the *most* important thing.

Which, when it all boils down to it, is this:

You've got this!

You really do.

'If you want to
go fast,
go alone.
If you want to
go far,
go together.'

African proverb

10

Find Your Uplift

Connect to people who help you rise

I will never forget the outpouring of love in the weeks and months following my brother Peter's death. I felt carried along by an invisible current of love; my whole family did.

Numerous times people asked me, 'How are you doing?'

I was sad, of course. Profoundly sad. Yet amid the sadness lay something beautiful: a sense of deep connectedness, of community, of compassion.

I told people that I felt 'lifted up' and 'carried along' by love. It sounded corny to my ears, yet it felt like truth. How does love lift us up? How does community carry us along? How does connectedness fuel our courage — not just in hard times, but at *all* times?

I don't know exactly how. I just know it does.

As Bishop Michael Curry said during his impassioned sermon at the wedding of Meghan Markle and Prince Harry: 'There is a power in love.'

I would expand this and say that there is a power in all human connection. That every genuinely caring relationship — whether between friends, colleagues, clients or mere neighbours — carries an invisible current of energy that exceeds the sum of the parts. A power that can lift us up and carry us further than we could ever go alone. Organisational psychologists refer to this as 'emotional contagion'; the transmission of energy from one person to the next which has the power to spread like a virus ... for better or for worse.

NEVER UNDERESTIMATE THE VALUE OF FRIENDSHIPS IN SURVIVING DIFFICULT TIMES.

I'm sure you've seen them flying overhead: a flock of geese moving across the sky in an elegant 'V' formation. As each bird flaps its wings, it creates uplift for the bird immediately following and reduces the amount of energy they have to expend. By flying together like this, they can extend their flying range to over 70 per cent more than they could if they flew alone. The regular 'honk honk' you may have heard is the geese encouraging those ahead to keep up their speed. When the lead goose tires, since it's the one not benefiting from the uplift effect, it rotates to the back of the 'V' where the resistance is lowest, and another goose takes point position up front. Should a goose fall out of formation, it quickly loses the uplift advantage and must flap harder to overcome the drag, so it tends to pretty quickly return back into formation.

When a goose gets sick, or is wounded and cannot stay in the formation, two other geese fall out with their companion and follow it down to provide help and protection. They stay with the fallen goose until it is able to fly, or it dies. Only then do they launch out to catch up with the group.

PEOPLE WHO WILL TELL YOU HARD TRUTHS, CHAMPION YOUR GREATNESS AND NEVER LET YOU MAKE A MOUNTAIN FROM A MOLEHILL ARE GOLD IN YOUR LIFE. TREASURE THEM ACCORDINGLY.

Researcher John Cacioppo from the University of Chicago found that as a social species, we access our greatest strength from our ability to plan, collaborate and communicate *together*, not from going it alone. A little like those geese. Likewise, when we lack meaningful relationships with people who give us 'uplift' and help us enjoy more positive emotions, our health suffers, we are unable to fly as far as we'd like and when life knocks us down, it's that much harder to pick ourselves back up.

Mastery of life is not a solo endeavour. Finding people to give you 'airlift', help you find your own 'true north' and reset your course when you lose your bearings is vital to your success, however you define it.

Studies find that loneliness has the same impact on mortality as smoking the fifteen cigarettes a day, making feelings of social disconnection even more dangerous than obesity. So prioritising your time to foster richer relationships with people who will help you thrive amid life's challenges isn't just a nice thing to do, it can literally add years to your life and life to your living. As I've found myself many times, having people around you who see your strengths, have got your back and support your success, make it that bit easier to venture out on a limb and trust your wings in the moments when it matter most.

When I embarked on writing my first book, *Find Your Courage*, I was too afraid to tell anyone for fear their responses might weaken my tenuous hold on courage. In the very beginning, only my husband, Andrew, who had pushed back on my misgivings about my literary skills (or lack thereof), knew I had taken the bold leap towards becoming an author. Without his encouragement to 'just write the best book you can', I might still be lingering in a swamp of doubt, waiting for the confidence to begin.

AUTHENTIC CONNECTIONS INSTIL IN US RESILIENCE THAT SURPASSES THE SUM OF OUR INDIVIDUAL PARTS.

Having relocated from Australia to Dallas, Texas, a few years earlier, no-one in my social orbit knew me BC (before children). To them, I was a stay-at-home mom of four young kids (six, five, three and one at the time). A few of my neighbours knew I was 'tinkering' in this new field called 'life coaching', yet I sensed they considered it to be a nice little side hobby; a harmless distraction from the hard yards of motherhood.

The truth was that my confidence in being able to forge a whole new career while also raising four children was pretty fragile. Between leaving the corporate world a few years earlier and then moving across the world to a country where I could count on one hand how many people I knew within a 10 000 mile radius, my identity as a professional was a little tenuous. With my inner critic stuck on replay asking (in a highly passive-aggressive tone) 'Who do you think you are to write a book?' I just couldn't risk someone — particularly the other stay-at-home mothers in the neighbourhood — making an offhand remark that would send me back to that 'doubt swamp'. Besides, I sensed that they'd think I was totally insane to even attempt to write a book when most of us were struggling to sit down and read one.

But it was imagining how I might feel at life's end if I didn't heed the tug on my heart that helped me find my own courage to get started.

Each afternoon after I'd wrangled my kids down for a nap, I'd 'steal' an hour (and on lucky days, two!) to sit at a small desk in the corner of my bedroom and write. As the months went by, something resembling a book began to emerge. Writing a book to help people living in the shadow of fear to 'find their courage' took every ounce of my own; it was my own 'coming out' in a way, my own brave act of defiance against the social norms around me.

FEAR IS CONTAGIOUS, BUT SO IS COURAGE. WE ARE BRAVER TOGETHER THAN WE CAN EVER BE ALONE.

Over that same period, I developed a friendship with Janet Johnston. Janet, a partner at a professional services firm, was one of the very few women I met locally who worked. I had asked Janet if she'd help me out by letting me coach her in order to get my coaching certification. After agreeing to be one of my first coaching 'guinea pig' clients, Janet went on to become a dear friend and one of my most ardent supporters, actively promoting me to her professional network, including opening the door to my first ever paid speaking engagement (I'll never forget the thrill and sense of affirmation of being paid $200 to give a talk after having done so many for free). Whenever we were out anywhere, Janet would tout my brilliance to anyone who cared to listen (and maybe a few who didn't). Often I'd feel embarrassed by how loudly she'd sing my praises. She'd just laugh at me and tell me I needed to own it. Needless to say, Janet was (and continues to be) someone I could count on for cheerleading. Sensing that she was 'safe' to bring into the fold on my authorial aspirations, I told her about my book. 'Of course you should write a book. Let me know when it's done. I'll buy a box,' she said. 'I'm sure it's going to be a bestseller and help millions!'

Looking back, it's clear that Janet's expectations for how successful that first book would be were a little (lot) optimistic. Yet her belief in me and in my work was immeasurably valuable at the time. When *Find Your Courage* eventually came out (self-published at first and then later re-released by a large US publisher), Janet helped me get uplift. Not only did she order that box, but (after getting me to autograph them, which added precisely zero to their resale value) she gave copies to a whole host of influencers and decision makers within her network. Her support opened up all sorts of new opportunities for me, and the ripple effect goes on to this day.

Andrew is a lifter.

Janet is a lifter.

So too are many of the big-hearted people I have spinning in my orbit, near and far. And I can honestly say that I would not be writing this book if they weren't. Their belief in me set me on a wholly different, and far braver, trajectory.

Human history tells us that we are wired for connection. The human species would not have survived without the instinctive desire to build relationships and create communities with those around us. The bonds we forge with others are an invaluable source of courage, of resilience, of strength. The Harvard Study, which I cited in the last chapter, found that the singular most important predictor of wellbeing and longevity is the strength of one's social network. Close relationships — more than money, fame, IQ, genes or social class — are what make people happiest throughout their lives, helping to ward off mental and physical decline and endure life's inevitable adversities. Numerous other clinical studies have backed this up: people with a strong support network recover from illness and injury faster, have lower cancer recurrence, report less loneliness and higher contentment, and age stronger with higher mobility longer into their life.

Which begs the question: Who's flying in your V?

EVERY HUMAN INTERACTION INVOLVES AN EXCHANGE OF ENERGY. TAKE FULL OWNERSHIP OF BOTH THE ENERGY YOU PUT OUT, AND THE ENERGY YOU LET IN.

Some say that you can tell how successful someone will be by looking at the five people they spend the most time with. Whether it's five or fifteen, the point is the same: who you spend time with has a profound impact on your outlook, your aspirations, your actions and, by default, the outcomes you create in your life.

Are you the biggest-thinking, most ambitious person in your social circle? Or do you hold back from even sharing your dreams for fear that others might react negatively? Do the people around you spend a lot of their time complaining, blaming, guilting or judging other people who are 'up to stuff' in their lives? Do you ever get bored of the conversations and long to talk about more meaningful things?

If you answered 'yes' to any of the above (much less to all of them) then consider the possibility that maybe, just maybe, you need to get out of that lovely social comfort zone of yours and make some new friends.

People who will push back on your doubts and cheer on your dreams.

People who will not buy into your worn-out excuses about why you can't.

People who will refuse to let you sell yourself short or play small.

People who are up to cool things and passionate about their life.

Most of all, people who will, in their own words and in their own way, reaffirm your self-belief that you've got this!

People like Jacinta McDonell.

I met Jacinta in New York where a group of women leaders and entrepreneurs had rendezvoused before flying to the British Virgin Islands where we were to spend five days with Richard Branson and a host of other leaders and luminaries. Of course, meeting someone as iconic as Richard Branson is a pretty cool experience. It was made even more special by the opportunity to interview him for those whom Virgin and Emma Isaacs, founder of Business Chicks, had brought together.

Yet the most impactful part of the whole experience for me was the generous-spirited, big-hearted and purpose-driven people I got to meet. Like Jacinta, who co-founded Australia's largest fitness franchise and later founded the Human Kind Project, a social venture aimed at applying commercial smarts to eradicating world hunger and supporting underprivileged communities. I've lost count now how many times, in the midst of wondering about what to do next, Jacinta has told me 'You've got this, babe', championed me to 'Go big or go home' or sent a short email to say 'I've got your back hun'.

Finding people like Jac will require being proactive in building new relationships and risking the odd rejection along the way. I've had a few. But that's okay, because not everyone is meant to fly in your flock, and you may not be meant for theirs. So be it. Wish them well. Move on.

What matters most is being intentional about being the kind of person others would want to hang out with and hanging out with the kind of people you want to be. Having moved around a lot, I have had to employ a lot of intentionality!

When I landed in Singapore, the local café economy got a boost from my many coffee meetings with all array of interesting people hailing from many countries, cultures and walks of life (diversity is one of the things I've loved most about living in Singapore). Friends of friends of friends' second cousins. Colleagues of colleagues of a colleague's former colleague. Ex-neighbours of former clients. The net was cast wide.

Six months in (and caffeinated out), I'd kindled numerous relationships with a diverse group of wonderful people. One of them was a human rights lawyer called Tamera Fillinger, whom I met when I arrived late to a parent luncheon at my sons' school. (I attempted to look inconspicuous by sitting at the table at the far back of the room ... which turned out to be the faculty table. But Tamera, who was on the school board, was seated beside me so it was one of those fortuitous mistakes.)

I loved Tamera's company and upbeat outlook on life, but between our work, family and travels we struggled to catch up near as often as we'd like to. So one afternoon, over a pot of tea in my apartment, we came up with the idea of starting a book club. We figured that, at a minimum, it would ensure we would see each other at least once a month and, all going well, a few other women could join us.

It will come as little surprise that I'm quite partial to non-fiction books that have anything to do with personal or professional development. So we called our new book club the 'Best-Self Book Club', with the only rule being that any books we read had to be related to something that would help us become a better version of ourselves. Some were on nutrition, money mindset

(*The Soul of Money*), mindful eating (anything by Geneen Roth), and others were on mindfulness, spirituality, ageing strong and living big. Like every book club, our conversations often stray a long (*looong*) way off topic, but these gatherings of thoughtful women are always food for the soul. While book clubs aren't everyone's cup of tea, I share this simply to encourage you to be creative in finding ways to spend more time with people who lift you up.

TRUE FRIENDS LIFT US UP WHEN OUR WINGS ARE STRUGGLING TO REMEMBER HOW TO FLY.

Like most people, I instinctively want people to think well of me; to think my life is relatively sorted. Or even just sort of sorted. But like most people, I've had more than my share of moments in which life has felt *anything* but sorted. Interesting? Yes. Sorted? Not even close. In fact with all the unexpected relocations and *plans-interruptus* (my home-crafted Latin translation for well-laid plans being turned abruptly on their head) that have landed me living *longwaytoofar* (one of my favourite Pidgin English phrases from Papua New Guinea) from my kids, I've felt life has been more unsorted than ever in recent years. Yet these 'plot twists' have just affirmed my belief that we forge far more meaningful connections through our vulnerability than through our victories, more through our struggles than our successes, more through our troubles than our triumphs.

Of course, often in the midst of our toughest times, when we feel most vulnerable and least together, our instincts are to wind up the drawbridge, withdraw from others and paint on a smiley face when we venture out. Yet this is precisely the time when lowering our masks and sharing our struggle with those who love us can be most helpful. Research may show that social connections are one of the strongest predictors of wellbeing, but those social connections are only as valuable as the authenticity we bring to them.

Our social media posts are our highlight reels. They don't portray the full reality of our lives. Accordingly, friendships built online are often as superficial as the posts we see. Lots of platitudes and selfies, little substance. Only when you pull back the curtain and let people into the offline reality of your life can you build truly meaningful relationships with real people who really, truly, have your back. Sadly, the data shows that today people have fewer meaningful relationships than 25 years ago. Little wonder the number one reason people seek counselling today is for loneliness. A study by Relate, a UK charity that provides relationship counselling services, found that one in ten people say they have no friends and one in five say they feel unloved.

As our online networks have grown more expansive our relationships have grown increasingly superficial. People are ever more connected but never more alone. Which is why you cannot rely solely on your Facebook friendships or Instagram followers to help you find your courage and conquer your doubts when life presses in. It's also why it's so vital to peel back the façade and let people into what's really going on when the chips are down. Relationships forged through shared adversity, vulnerability and authenticity will be infinitely stronger than those built on trading selfie likes.

PEOPLE HAVE NEVER BEEN MORE CONNECTED, YET FELT SO ALONE. THE MORE WIRED YOUR LIFE, THE MORE DELIBERATE YOU MUST BE TO UNPLUG AND DEEPEN YOUR RELATIONSHIPS OFFLINE.

Maybe it's my country girl 'take me as you see me' upbringing, but on the spectrum of closed book to open book, I tend to lean towards the open book side. A few times this has left me with a 'vulnerability hangover' — a term coined by Brené Brown that describes that deep sick feeling in your gut when you've exposed yourself to the full judgement of others (not dissimilar to how I felt when I locked myself out of my hotel room in my underpants!).

Earlier in my career my openness caused me some grief when, a few weeks into a new job, I was too honest and transparent with one of my new colleagues, who was older than me by about five years but in a more junior position. Since it hadn't occurred to me that she might be envious of me for being hired into a more senior position despite being less experienced, I shared quite openly some of my frustrations about our manager. Unbeknownst to me she promptly told others on the team what I'd shared, including the manager! Needless to say, it was a hard lesson: not everyone has earned your truth and trust; not everyone deserves your vulnerability. If you've been similarly burnt, don't overreact by closing down.

Having the courage to share what's truly going on for you with those who *are* deserving of your trust allows you to forge far more real and rewarding relationships than you ever could by only holding your cards tightly to your chest or limiting your exchanges to ten-word text messages.

WE ARE AT OUR STRONGEST WHEN WE CONNECT FROM THE DEEPEST PART OF OURSELVES WITH THE DEEPEST PART OF OTHERS.

A useful litmus test — if something really crappy happened to you and you woke this person up at 3 in the morning for support, would they happily give up their sleep to help you out? If that is just a bar too high, then what if you called this person at 3 in the afternoon to help you out, would they happily do whatever they could? If you get nervous about the very thought of actually calling them at all because you only ever text, then you've got your answer right there.

The redwood trees of California grow hundreds of feet into the sky and many are over 2000 years old. How have these trees withstood the ravages of time and nature for so long? Growing in thick groves, they are all connected through a vast underground root system, sometimes extending over 30 metres from the trunk, where the roots intertwine, sometimes even fusing together.

Nature holds many lessons for us humans, and these redwoods are no exception. So if you're struggling with a situation right now, identify whom you can reach out to and share the raw and sometimes messy 'un-Photoshopped' truth of your life. Just as not everyone is a worthy confidant, not everyone will be capable of responding with compassion. Some people are too caught up in their own 'stuff' to have any capacity to empathise with yours. So be discerning, but don't just soldier on alone.

A couple of years ago we decided as a family to climb Mount Kilimanjaro. Now, before you start thinking that mine is a 'von Trapp'–style mountain-climbing family, let me disabuse you of that notion. Prior to kids, Andrew and I had hiked the Inca Trail in Peru, climbed Mount Cotopaxi in Ecuador and summited Mount Wilhelm in Papua New Guinea. However, by the time we decided to climb Kilimanjaro with our four kids — aged thirteen, fourteen, seventeen and eighteen at the time — I had long since lost/misplaced/donated my hiking boots and the kids didn't own any. We also lived at sea level so we were anything but regular mountain climbers. However, with Andrew's fiftieth birthday on the horizon and, inspired by a motivational slide deck Ben put together to pitch the idea (complete with *Rocky* soundtrack), we figured it would be a great way to mark his half century so I got to work organising the logistics. As I did, a few friends who were more seasoned climbers questioned the decision, pointing out that many people don't make it to the top and that, without a pretty serious training regime, we needed to prepare ourselves (and the kids' expectations) that we would be among those who'd turn around long before reaching the summit, which stands nearly six kilometres (19 340 feet) above the African plains below.

OUR FULFILMENT OCCURS THROUGH OUR RELATIONSHIP WITH OTHERS. LIFT AS YOU CLIMB — WE ALL RISE HIGHER WHEN WE'RE PULLING EACH OTHER UP.

After learning that altitude can have a magnified impact on younger people, we opted for the longer Rongai route, taking four full days to get to base camp to give our bodies time to acclimatise. On reaching base camp at 4700 metres (15 400 feet) into the African sky, we realised it was colder than our shoddy rental gear was equipped to handle so we spent most of the time in our small tents. Our guides woke us up early on 'summit day' so we could get cracking well before dawn. The idea was to reach the rim by sunrise. Huh. Little did we realise, we would not even come remotely close to that.

Within 30 minutes Matthew (recently turned thirteen) was in tears, his fingers so cold in his shabby gloves that they were really hurting. I felt like crying too as mine were also freezing, but figured I needed to show a little stoicism so early in the climb. Within another 30 minutes Ben (fourteen) was throwing up the oatmeal he'd eaten before embarking on our arduous ascent. *Not a good start*, I thought. But we plodded along '*poli poli*' as they say in Swahili, meaning 'slowly slowly'. During the first few hours, we stopped every five minutes or so to drink some water under the dark night sky. Yet the higher we climbed into the African sky, and the less oxygen we inhaled with each breath, the more frequent those breaks became and the slower our steps in between.

I felt nauseated and my head pounded. About five hours in and with the rim appearing to get further and further away, my nausea reached the point that I threw up the one protein bar I'd managed to eat. I kept sipping on water and with each break I would literally lay my head back on the ground and fall into what I can only call a 'nano-nap'.

Numerous times, I thought to myself *Why on earth did we ever do this*? Ben, whose idea it had been to begin with, later said he thought the same, kicking himself for the flashy slide deck he'd created to sell us all on the idea. Unlike the four previous days where we'd hiked along singing songs, telling jokes and engaging in family banter, we hardly spoke a word as every bit of energy went into simply putting one foot in front of the other as we zigzagged up the moonlike landscape of the soft shale mountainside, much of it a little like climbing up a sand dune.

The last few hundred metres to the top were the most brutal. As our small steps grew smaller, so too did the intervals between our stops to swig some water and catch our breath. (The kids all say it was me that slowed everyone down, but I didn't see anyone complaining.) When we finally reached the top, nine gruelling hours after setting out, there were no cheers of elation, just exhausted silence. Matthew lay on a large boulder, taking in a few rays of the sun's warmth. I recall assembling us all together to get a photo as our guides, Dawson, Frank and Stephen, high-fived each other with beaming smiles, delighted they'd got us all to the top. It had most certainly not been a given (we later learnt the porters who'd helped carry supplies up the mountain had been quite sceptical about all six of us reaching the summit). At thirteen, Matthew was not the youngest person to climb Kilimanjaro, but he was only a few years older than the child who was.

Summiting Mt Kilimanjaro was the most physically gruelling day of my life. What kept me moving forward, *poli poli*, was the fact that we were all in it together. On numerous occasions, when one of us would fall down in an exhausted heap, the others would come over and extend a hand to lift them up. 'Come on, you can do it,' we'd be saying to each other. 'Just a few more steps and we'll have another break.'

We did not climb Kilimanjaro as individuals. We climbed as a family, a team, our own little flock of geese (as the oxygen thinned, Andrew was the one left paving the trail at the front). It was our collective commitment to climbing together on the rooftop of Africa, marking Andrew's birthday as a family, that kept any of us from giving up, as tempting as that was. The power of our collective effort in Africa speaks to this wonderful African proverb: If you want to go fast, go alone. If you want to go far, go together.

The value of lifting others as you climb holds as true for scaling a mountain as it does for pursuing any meaningful goal. Taking the focus off yourself and doing something to encourage someone else — whether to lend your support, to cheer them on or to simply let them know that you're thinking of them and you've got their back — doesn't just lift them, it lifts you too. Research has found that when we do something kind for someone else, it actually releases feel-good hormones in our own systems that benefit us as well as those who were on the receiving end of our generosity. But it doesn't even end there. People who witness our kindness also benefit. To quote Ralph Waldo Emerson, 'It is one of the beautiful compensations in this life that no one can sincerely try to help another without helping himself.'

BE THE KIND OF PERSON YOU WANT TO HANG OUT WITH AND HANG OUT WITH THE KIND OF PEOPLE YOU'D LIKE TO BE.

I often write articles or film videos that I share through my newsletters and social media channels to encourage people to act bravely amid their doubts, fears and uncertainty. People regularly tell me that what I've shared came at the perfect time. Some ask if I've been stalking them, as I seem to have spoken about their exact situation. What they often don't realise is that I tend to write about whatever I'm struggling with myself. Which just goes to show that, while the specifics of our struggles are different, the larger dynamics are universal. It's why I'm writing this book. Because there've been many times I've appreciated people reminding me 'You've got this.' And I'm guessing there's many times you've wanted to hear it too. Maybe right now.

The reality is that the more you act as the kind of person others want in their corner, the more you attract the kind of people who you would want in yours. It begins with *you*. Look around you and ask yourself who in your orbit could do with your support — whether it be grabbing a coffee with them or forwarding on a TED talk you found inspiring or a link to an event you think they might like to attend.

When my friend Suzi Pomerantz, a veteran in the coaching profession, heard I was running my first Live Brave (un)retreat in North America, she immediately reached out to offer her support. I confided to her how my vulnerability meter had dialed up to a solid ten as I started the marketing and contacting people in my networks to help spread the word. She just said, 'Oh honey, you are so brave. I hope you know, you've totally got this.' Her words of faith in me were like gold. I let them soak in and bolster my own faith, which was definitely in need of reinforcement.

Having great people around you is so important when you're venturing out of your comfort zone and your doubts are more likely to rear their noisy heads. They were in full volume again recently the morning I was to deliver the closing keynote at a large conference for professional speakers. I had never spoken to an audience of speakers before, and was well aware of how talented and experienced many of them were. While I knew they'd be a supportive group, my stomach was a tangle of butterflies as there's something particularly nerve-racking about speaking to people who are spinning in the same professional orbit. To make it even more nerve-racking, I was fresh off the plane from a lot of international travel in the weeks leading up to the conference and I'd not managed to do the level of preparation that would have been ideal.

'This is in your wheelhouse,' my friend Paul messaged me that morning as I was trying (in vain) to get my butterflies flying in formation. I knew he was right, but, at the moment his affirming words landed on my phone, I really appreciated someone else reminding me. And while I'd like to think I might one day outgrow the need for external affirmation, I'm not there yet. (And the truth: I think none of us are.)

Having people around us who see our gifts, trust in our abilities and have got our backs should we falter, can make all the difference in those moments when our fear of being exposed as inadequate peaks. That day, I did falter a little as I walked onto the stage, and the clicker for my slides was acting a little clunky. But then I hit my stride, got into flow and, by the end, people felt inspired enough to stand to applaud. It was pretty surreal. Yet it was also testament to the power we can tap into when those around us believe in us.

LIFT AS YOU CLIMB

Bring to mind the people who have been most affirming for you over the years.

Those people you've grown to count on to lift you up or cheer you on when you need a little encouragement or someone to confide in.

Those people who won't judge you for having doubts, or shame you for slipping up.

Those people who won't give up on you when times are tough and when you fall short of being the person you most want to be.

Who are they? If you have a pen in your hand right now, jot down their names.

But don't stop there. Make a point of reaching out to them — with a call, an email or, particularly meaningful in today's digital age, with a handwritten card. Let them know the impact they've had on your life, how grateful you are to them, what you admire most about them ... or whatever will touch them most!

This is an exercise I often have people do at my Live Brave programs, and attendees later told me that their handwritten cards have brought tears of joy to those who've received them. So don't underestimate the impact that just a few words of appreciation could make on the day, heart, and even the life, of someone who has enriched your own.

It doesn't matter how successful somebody is; everyone loves affirmation of the positive mark their life has made on another.

NEVER LET THE FEAR THAT LIVES IN OTHERS
SET UP RESIDENCE IN YOU. HEAR PEOPLE OUT,
BUT TRUST IN YOURSELF.

When a flower doesn't bloom, you don't blame the flower. You look at the environment in which it's growing, the size of the pot, the quality of the soil, the amount of sun it's getting. And then you change what's stifling its growth and keeping it from blossoming to its full brilliance.

Likewise, if you aren't blooming or at least moving in that general direction (we're not all early bloomers!), take a look at the people around you. They are your container, your soil, your sunlight.

I suspect you've encountered a few people in your life who you would not describe in the same sentence as sunlight. But just as you need to take 100 per cent responsibility for the energy you put out to others, so too you must take 100 per cent responsibility for the energy you let in.

Of course, not everyone will tell you how wonderful you are and encourage you to shoot for the stars. Not everyone will be there for you at 3 am when your heart is aching. And not everyone will cheer you on when you share that you want to make a significant change in your life (particularly if it affects them). And that's perfectly okay. Maybe they just have too much going on in their own lives.

But don't ignore or discount the impact on your own mindset and life experience of spending a lot of time with people you cannot count on to celebrate your wins, push back on your doubts, or encourage you to think bigger about yourself and what's possible. Every hour you spend with someone who is not bringing out your best and championing your bravest is an hour you could have been spending with someone who would.

Of course you don't always have a choice about whether or not to spend time with doomsayers and 'energy vampires'. Maybe you have to work with them, spend holidays with them, manage them, report to them. Maybe you're living with one.

In these cases, you need to be intentional about establishing barriers so that you don't let their doubts, fears, anxieties and insecurities become your own. Emotions are, after all, contagious. As Daniel Goleman wrote in *Emotional Intelligence*, 'Fear is like second hand smoke. It makes casual bystanders victims of others' toxic emotions.'

DON'T TREAT PEOPLE HOW THEY TREAT YOU. TEACH PEOPLE HOW TO TREAT YOU.

We can never change other people, but we can change how we engage with them. This requires overcoming our innate desire to be liked, preserve social harmony and make everyone around us feel happy. Sometimes you've got to set boundaries even if it risks getting some off-side. Experience has taught me that the only people who get upset when others set boundaries are those who'd been benefiting from their lack of boundaries.

Be compassionate, be kind, but not at the expense of doing what you need to do to ensure that you can grow and thrive. You can't pour from an empty cup. The best way to support those who have yet to confront their insecurities and face their fears is by showing up as someone who is confronting their own. After all, when people spread negative emotional contagion — whether they be cynical, judgemental, intolerant, pessimistic, anxious, spiteful, petty, arrogant — they are simply acting from a belief system that is mired in scarcity, insecurity and an unfulfilled need to prove their significance and validate their worthiness.

Be mindful that some people in your orbit might feel threatened by your desire to do something new or make something more of your life. If people react negatively (or even with a lack of enthusiasm) to your plans and aspirations, it's often got nothing to do with you and everything to do with how they feel about themselves. In which case, you don't do anyone a favour by dimming yourself down so as not to shine too brightly around those who've yet to trust their own light.

In the end, you shape your flock and your flock shapes you! The people showing up in your life are a reflection of what you're putting out. And vice versa.

You may have seen David Attenborough's documentary about the Emperor penguins of Antarctica who huddle together through the long bleak winter on the world's most southern icecap when temperatures drop to the coldest on the planet ... and stay there ... for months. They may have thick skin, but only by standing together can they survive the world's harshest conditions.

Geese. Penguins. People.

When we lean on each other we can stand stronger in the storms, and when we lift each other, we can rise higher, fly further and bounce back faster than we ever could going it alone.

So lean into those around you — be real, be vulnerable, be yourself.

And lift those around you — be generous, be compassionate, be encouraging.

Just minimise your time with those who don't lift you.

Honk honk.

'Embrace
uncertainty.
Some of the most
beautiful chapters in
our lives won't have
a title until much
later.'

Bob Goff

11
Surrender Resistance
Embrace the struggle and transform yourself

Just over two years ago I was readying myself to pack up my home and family in Australia to relocate back to the USA, where we'd previously lived for eleven years. Based on strong assurances of being relocated back to Andrew's company's 'mother ship', we'd sent our oldest two children — Lachlan and Maddy — back ahead of us to boarding school, something we'd never considered before as, quite frankly, we love having our kids around. Our younger two — Ben and Matthew — were also enrolled in schools for the fall and excited to reconnect with old friends.

And then one rainy morning in late April the phone rang. It was Andrew. 'Are you sitting down? You might want to.' My stomach tightened. I took a breath and sat.

Plans had changed. His company now wanted him in Singapore.

Singapore?!*!#?!

This was not in my plans. Not in any remotest plan.

After picking myself up from the ground and soaking a few friends' shoulders, I decided to move on from my own little pity party (my default go-to response) and dub it as a 'plot twist'. I figured changing my language around it would help me to reframe relocating my family, business and career to yet another continent as one more chapter in the grand adventure of life.

While no move is easy (we've lived in fourteen homes since getting married), this one was the toughest by far. Not only was I not getting back on the same continent as my oldest two children, making up for the precious lost time with them, but I had to pull my youngest two children (fourteen and fifteen at the time) out of school midway through the Australian school year to relocate to a country that they'd previously declared zero interest in even visiting. To add to the challenge, we were unable to get both boys into the same school as we were so late to the enrolment process. Then to up the ante some more, Matthew was placed in the wrong year level (right academically, wrong socially). When he was two weeks in and absolutely miserable, it took hard lobbying on my part to have him moved up a year against the advice of pretty much every educator we spoke to (but which turned out well for him, making a strong case to trust parental instinct!).

Despite our best efforts, Matthew never took to Singapore. After a year of begging and pleading with us to let him go to boarding school, we eventually acquiesced. It was one of the hardest parenting decisions I'd ever had to make but we ultimately decided to trust our fifteen-year-old's conviction that he was far better suited to a different educational environment.

And then ... another plot twist.

Just a month after the most emotionally wrenching school drop-off of my life, leaving my youngest child in boarding school on the other side of the world, Andrew was assigned to another role that meant he'd be away from Singapore more often than he was in it. But with Ben having only eighteen months left of high school, and no path (or visa) to move back to the US, the only real option was for me to stay in Singapore with him. And so our family unit became even more dispersed. Two teens at college in New York. One teen boarding in California. One teen in Singapore. To say this was never part of any family vision is an understatement.

Argggh.

Life is what happens when you're making other plans, right?

Well it just so happened that my fourth book, *Make Your Mark*, was released the month before this plot twist. And it just so happened that Step 5 of my '*7 Step Guidebook For Getting Unstuck & On Course To Make Your Biggest Mark*' was titled 'Lean into Life's Curves'. The opening paragraph read as follows.

Life doesn't happen to you, it happens for you.

Every disappointment, every derailed plan,

is really just a silent invitation,

for living deeper,

and growing wiser.

Life is not linear.

By leaning into its curves,

you discover its gold.

Now, you might assume that by the time an author pens such advice, it comes so naturally that they no longer need to work at practising it.

Not true.

Well, not true for *this* author! It's a heck of a lot easier to dish out advice than to follow it. So I've returned to that paragraph many times as I've dug deep into my own courage and tried to walk my own 'brave talk' these last couple of years.

And you know what I've found as I've road tested my own best advice?

It's solid.

And so as I write this now, I am happy to report that I'm doing well.

No, change that, I'm doing better than well. In fact, I've never felt stronger.

Is the uncertainty gone? Nope.

Is life still messy, my family still scattered across the globe, and the ground beneath me still wobbly? You bet.

But you know what? I've come to know something about myself on a soul-deep level.

No matter what happens, I can figure it out.

More so, that my children and Andrew and those I love can also figure it out. That no matter how undefined the path ahead, we will be okay. Even when things are not as we'd like and the future we planned and sacrificed for isn't the one that arrived. (Well not *yet*, but we sure haven't given up hope!)

Of course, I'd love to also tell you that I have been the walking embodiment of grace through this entire period. That I have been eternally supportive of my husband. That I have never railed at our situation and no disgruntled remarks have left my lips about the lack of empathy or leadership courage of some who have risen in his company. That I've not endured a single moment of angst about having my four children in their adolescent and early adult years living much further (like 15 000 kilometres further) away from me than I'd have liked.

But of course, I cannot. I'd hate to count up all the moments my stomach has felt queasy or the restless nights I've tossed and turned trying to figure out the best path forward.

Yet, by fate or good fortune, my work has drawn me down a few serendipitous paths over this same period. Not only did I launch my podcast I have ~~shamelessly plugged~~ referenced numerous times throughout this book, but I also began a PhD in the dynamics of power, gender and leadership (perhaps another book?). Both endeavours have opened valuable opportunities to widen the lens through which I've been able to observe and understand this experience. It's helped me, when life has felt most ungrounded, to become grounded in myself.

Numerous times on this winding journey friends have said, 'You've got this Margie.' I doubt they realised quite how hungry I was for their affirming words; how much I needed to lean on the faith they had that I'd figure my way out of the mess and, together with Andrew, find a way to transform these 'plot twists' into catalysts for our own growth, helping make ourselves and our family unit stronger for it.

After all, adversity has a way of introducing us to parts of ourselves we might never encounter otherwise. It's why we grow far more from difficult times than easy ones. That said, no-one says it's a walk in the park when you're slam in the middle of it. It's why holding on to faith that those dots will connect is so mission critical when you wonder if the universe is conspiring against you!

You may have heard of the five stages of grief that psychiatrist Elisabeth Kübler-Ross identified: Denial. Anger. Depression. Bargaining. Acceptance.

Since her book *On Death and Dying* was published in 1969, experts have found that these five stages are not sequential, but non-linear states that people move back and forth between. As Sheryl Sandberg wrote in *Option B* after the sudden loss of her husband, 'Grief and anger aren't extinguished like flames doused in water. They can flicker away one moment and burn hot the next.'

While we all process loss in our own unique way, there is a general consensus among experts that denial is always the first state we move into in the aftermath of any form of significant loss. Loss of plans. Loss of people. Loss of place. Loss of external anchors to bolster our sense of safety, security, certainty.

STOP FIGHTING REALITY. THE BIGGEST THING THAT MESSES US UP IS THE PICTURE IN OUR HEADS OF HOW WE THINK LIFE SHOULD BE.

While denial can be a healthy coping mechanism in the aftermath of great loss, it can also keep us stuck and cripple our ability to move forward. Denying reality sets us on a collision course with reality, one that can hurl us into a downward spiral of blame, bitterness, self-pity and despair.

It can't be this way. It's not right. It's not possible. This just doesn't happen to me! This is BS. I don't believe it. It's not true. It can't be true.

And yet it is.

We all live in what psychologists call an 'assumptive world'. When something happens that 'cannot happen' in the world we've created in our heads, we fight back. It's rarely pretty. More often than not we just create for ourselves a whole lot of needless suffering. In fact, it's a core tenet of Buddhism that all suffering comes from our attachment to how we think things *should* be. And let's face it, it's Murphy's Law that our ideas about how life should be almost never aligns with how life actually is.

What you resist persists. Putting up a fight against 'what is' doesn't make it go away. In fact it just wears you out and grinds you down and leaves you feeling bruised and battered and at odds with the world. Which, in case it isn't obvious, is a real party wrecker and joy sucker. It also keeps you from finding, and making, the best of whatever your new reality may be.

Chinese handcuffs, sometimes called Chinese finger traps, are comprised of a small cylinder of woven straw or paper into which the forefingers are placed at either end. The harder you pull, the tighter your fingers are held. Legend has it that emperors would select their officials based on how they responded to these 'finger cuffs'. Some responded by getting frustrated and resisting hard, thereby tightening the trap around their fingers. Those who remained calm were able to loosen the grip of the trap and escape it. The former were deemed unsuitable for leadership roles, while the latter passed the test. The lesson: if railing at your situation isn't improving it, you might want to try another tack. Just sayin'.

TRUST THAT SOMETHING WILL GROW FROM YOUR SETBACKS AND STRUGGLES. IT WILL BE YOU.

Now if you've ever heard me speak, you've probably heard me caution against the 'path of least resistance' and extol the virtues of the road less travelled — doing what's right over what's easy, what's truthful over what's comfortable.

However, I have a caveat.

This only applies when you have a choice about the path. In which case, have the courage to choose the road less travelled if that path feels right for you. However, when you *don't* have a choice — when you cannot change your situation — it's far wiser to choose the path of least resistance by letting go your resistance to the path.

In other words, choose the path that's been chosen for you.

Instead of wasting your energy on an unwinnable war, you can rechannel it into making the most of your new situation — seizing the yet unseen opportunities it holds. As Napoleon Hill once wrote, 'In every adversity lays the seed of an equal or greater benefit.' Your challenge is doing what you can to help those seeds sprout and being patient while they do.

(Patience has never been my strong suit. Just ask my kids.)

The other upside of giving up your fight is that you remove the source of your suffering. My case in point — I didn't want to move to Singapore but, despite the thousands of air miles I've clocked, and moments with my kids I've missed, I've absolutely thrived living in the culturally diverse and dynamic

'Little Red Dot' (as Singapore is often called). It has enriched my experience as a human being and broadened my perspective on the world, on other cultures and on the future. Singapore may seem too clean, controlled and orderly for some, but I've found it to be a welcoming vibrant melting pot brimming with enterprising global citizens who see the world through a broad lens.

My time living in Asia has validated the words of Ellen Langer, a professor at Harvard, whom I met a few years back: 'Every situation can be turned into a win if we shift our focus.'

Complaining about what you cannot change holds you hostage to old plans, old dreams, and old 'mental maps' of how the world *should* be. Yet who says your grand plans were a masterstroke of genius anyway? Maybe, just maybe, what's coming around the corner eclipses any plans that you could have cooked up for yourself. So be careful you don't miss out on the doors that are opening because you're so preoccupied and riled about the ones that closed.

WHEN YOU EMBRACE YOUR LIFE FOR ALL THAT IT IS, YOU RECLAIM THE ENERGY LOST TO THE BATTLE AGAINST WHAT IT ISN'T.

Consider the possibility that in this moment right now nothing is actually wrong. I mean, what if every circumstance of your life today that you thought was a problem actually held a silent invitation intended to serve your highest good? Not your highest comfort levels. Not your greatest convenience. Not your biggest bank balance (no, definitely not that!). But for the greatest good of the person you have it within you to become. And for the good that you might do in the world, and the lives of others, that would never be done if not for the storms you'd weathered.

If pondering this perspective even remotely dislodges any negativity festering away within you, then maybe there's something to it.

Buddhist monk Thich Nhat Hanh once wrote that it is not impermanence that makes us suffer. What makes us suffer is wanting things to be permanent when they are not. So if you are struggling with the fact that something in your world has shifted in a direction you don't much like, consider what it is about your life right now, today, that you are not savouring fully given that it too, one day, will be gone.

To experience the richness of life, to dive deep into its waters and to avoid the perils of living only in its shallows, we must embrace its inherent impermanence, and open our hearts wide to whatever each moment holds — for all that it is and, every bit as importantly, for all that it isn't. No *thing* is permanent. Every *thing* eventually falls away. Our children will grow up and leave home. Our parents die. Our firm bodies soften (mine did this at thirteen). Our vision dims.

During the final stages of writing this book, my father-in-law passed away. Chris' health had been failing over the last year or two and we knew he was in the twilight of his life. A week before his passing his health took a steep dive and we knew his death was imminent. Yet when Andrew rang to tell me his dad had just drawn his last breath, Andrew by his bedside, I was still unprepared for the finality of it all. On dealing with the death of those we love, many have shared with me similar experiences. While we intellectually understand our bodies are mortal, a part of us still grapples to accept this fundamental truth ...

Because life is the way it is, it cannot stay the way it is.

Anything we cannot control is teaching us to let go. So don't wait until the ground feels fully solid beneath you. Rather, feel grounded in yourself and step forward to whatever is calling you. Because those windows of opportunity that you see right now, they too shall one day close. And that surge of life energy beating within you, that too shall one day end. As Elisabeth Kübler-Ross wrote, 'it is the denial of death that is partially responsible for people living empty, purposeless lives; for when you live as if you'll live forever, it becomes too easy to postpone the things you know that you must do.'

Change, even change for the better, is innately uncomfortable. It's why we so often try to avoid it, or resist it or deny it and lull ourselves into a false sense of temporary security. Yet clinging to things as they are now — a job, a relationship, a daily routine or lifestyle — can leave you in a less secure and more vulnerable place one or five or ten years from now than if you were to be proactive in embracing whatever changes are coming your way. Dare I say, even pursuing them; throwing your arms and heart wide open to the adventure life truly is.

Leaving my parents' farm at eighteen. Backpacking around the world at 21. Crossing the Sahara and travelling around the Middle East alone at 23. Moving to Papua New Guinea at 26. Moving to the US weeks after 9/11 with three small children at 32. Not one of these experiences was comfortable. Countless times I felt apprehensive, unsure of my next step (or where I'd next lay my head), longing for the familiarity I'd left behind.

Yet by embracing change as a constant in my life, I've come to learn at the deepest level that I don't need to know exactly what the future holds in order to feel grounded. I just need to know myself. Along with that, I just need to trust myself, my resourcefulness and resilience, my values and vision, and to have faith that whatever unfolds, I'll be okay. The next step will reveal itself as I need to take it (though sometimes not a moment before).

TRUE SECURITY CAN ONLY BE FOUND BY LOOKING WITHIN. SEARCHING OUTSIDE YOURSELF WILL ONLY MAKE YOU LESS SECURE, NOT MORE SO.

The research bears this out. Studies have found that people whose conviction is built on internal values — integrity, community, self-acceptance, courage, purpose, compassion — have a greater sense of self-certainty that they can lean into when their lives are unpredictable (as distinct from external values like money, image, fame).

A study at Stanford University validated 'attitude certainty' as a form of psychological safety net that can bolster our self-trust. Before going into a negotiation, they broke people into two groups. One was primed to feel strong conviction in their internal values, and the other wasn't primed at all. Those who'd reconnected with their core beliefs and values (those that align with the 'true self') remained more confident of success, experienced less doubt and felt more self-assured in their talents and abilities. Recommitting to your deepest internal values helps you stay grounded in yourself when life feels shaky.

No matter how momentous the changes occurring in your world right now — whether by choice or by chance — you have everything within you to regain your own footing and stay grounded in your innate capacity and power to meet the challenges of the changes ahead. So plug in with the 'uplifters' around you. Plug in to the values that anchor you. And plug in to the spirit within you. Because, as spiritual teacher Ram Dass wrote, 'As long as you think that what you are looking for is outside of yourself, it will never be enough.'

LIVE YOUR LIFE AS THE IMPROV ACT IT IS. TRUST THE EBB AND FLOW AND ROLL WITH THE PUNCHES. IF YOU HAVEN'T HAD ONE LATELY, IT'S COMING.

Life is far more an improv act than a Broadway play, regardless of how meticulous a script you've written. So sure, set your ideal end point and work towards it. But don't get hung up on the details as you move along. When you accept that you have to make life up as you go, it spares you a whole world of pain. It also liberates you to respond with a degree of mental and emotional agility you never could otherwise. My friend Rosie Batty's story is a powerful case in point.

When Rosie's son, Luke, was eleven years old, her estranged partner decided to use him as the ultimate weapon to hurt her. He killed his son, brutally. It is impossible to imagine how you'd react if your worst nightmare became your reality. Totally consumed by grief — beyond anything she could ever have imagined — Rosie spent the first days, and weeks, waiting to wake up and discover it was all a terrible nightmare. Except it wasn't. Her world had imploded. Her precious son had been taken from her, killed in a way that she was scarcely able to comprehend.

As the media gathered by her home, Rosie managed to compose herself enough to make a statement that won her the admiration of people across Australia, and eventually led to her being nominated Australian of the Year (the first Australian without a former public identity to receive the honour).

'Luke's father loved him,' she said.

If anything comes out of this, I want it to be a lesson to everybody that family violence happens to everybody no matter how nice your house is, no matter how intelligent you are, it happens to anyone and everyone.

Somehow in the midst of her devastation Rosie was able to find compassion for the man who had inflicted a wound on her heart that time can never fully erase. When I spoke to Rosie five years after Luke's death, she shared how she is still processing her loss, and learning to sit with her sorrow. Yet from the beginning she was determined not to be swallowed up by her grief and to find lightness in the ordinary moments of life.

Rosie's story is as unique as it is universal. You and I may never have to bear such heart-wrenching loss, but we will all bear loss that wrenches our hearts. The wisdom Rosie gained from having endured what many would say was unendurable holds a lesson for us all. As Rosie shared with me over a cup of tea at her kitchen table,

> *We can never underestimate the strength of the human spirit. We may feel utterly crushed but within us is a force that can rise again, even from the darkest times.*

Her wisdom brings to mind yet another favourite poem by Rumi:

> *This being human is a guest house.*
> *Every morning a new arrival.*
> *A joy, a depression, a meanness,*
> *some momentary awareness comes*
> *As an unexpected visitor.*
> *Welcome and entertain them all*
> *even if they're a crowd of sorrows,*
> *who violently sweep your house*
> *empty of its furniture,*
> *still treat each guest honourably.*
> *He may be clearing you out*
> *for some new delight.*
> *The dark thought, the shame, the malice,*
> *meet them at the door laughing and invite them in.*
> *Be grateful for whoever comes,*
> *because each has been sent*
> *as a guide from beyond.*

Sometimes opening our heart to the full catastrophe of life's muddled, messy and sometimes heart-wrenchingly raw emotions can take us beyond the boundaries of what we felt we could ever endure. After all, we aren't wired for pain; we're wired to avoid it. Yet moving away from what hurts us — by denying it, numbing it, avoiding it, disassociating from it — also cuts us off from what can heal our pain; from what would allow us to grow into a more whole-hearted person than we ever could otherwise.

IT'S NOT THE LOAD YOU CARRY, BUT HOW YOU CARRY IT.

Your emotions are neither right nor wrong. Rather they are part and parcel of what makes us human; an integral thread woven into the human condition. You might want to hide away in cave in the foothills of Tibet, but wherever you go, you take yourself with you. So wherever you go, sooner or later, you'll find yourself wrangling with emotions you tried to escape. So take heed of Rumi's words, and welcome them into your guest house, and let them be your teacher. What are they pointing you to pay attention to? The emotions we don't want to own will own us. Having the courage to fully feel your feelings is what allows them to move through you and not set up permanent residence in your psyche where they eventually express themselves in destructive ways, like growing an ulcer. Or worse.

I learnt this lesson most profoundly after a terrible motorbike accident left my brother Frank living in a wheelchair. As I wrote about in my book *Brave*, Frank was determined not to give his paraplegia the power to ruin his life. Change it, sure. Profoundly. But not to ruin it. His fierce determination to focus on what he could do, not on what he couldn't, brought home to me how easy it is for those of us with legs that work perfectly fine to get stuck living in mental wheelchairs of our own making — at war with our reality, dwelling on what we *cannot* do, not on what we can; on what we *don't* have, not on all we do — our futures confined by the mental cages we lock ourselves into.

Grief. Anger. Fear. Disappointment. Rejection.

Whatever emotions may rise up in you, trust in yourself that the only way out is through. And trust that however bad it feels right now, it won't feel this bad forever. In fact research shows that, most of the time, we overestimate how bad we'll feel at a future point in time. Even the deepest of grief eventually loosens its grip. So too with every other emotion.

HOWEVER BAD THINGS FEEL NOW, THEY WON'T FEEL THIS BAD FOREVER.

Any upset we feel constricts somewhere in your body. So a powerful way to process any painful emotion is to connect with where it is showing up in your body and to sit with the discomfort rather than to avoid it.

Is something upsetting you right now? If so, take a breath and notice where in your body it's showing up ... tightness in your chest, a sick feeling in your belly, a clenched jaw, a headache or aching back. Breathe into where you are feeling tightness or tingling, numbness or nausea. Holding your hand on that part of your body, breathe deeply right into that spot, and continue to breathe into it. Acknowledge the feeling, connect with the physical sensation. Keep breathing until you notice a gradual easing. It may not go away entirely, but it will loosen. And of course if it's something that's been plaguing you for a long time, consider engaging a professional to help you or doing a guided meditation to feel and heal your emotions. There are many online.

Indian sage Nisargadatta Maharaj wrote, 'We are not in our bodies, our bodies are in us.' Uncomfortable feelings in our body will never be comfortable, but the more often you allow yourself to feel uncomfortable feelings, the more comfortable you get with them and the sooner they loosen their hold, liberating you to move forward more grounded in your innate capacity to handle whatever life brings. It's a profoundly powerful place to live from. After all, when you know you can handle anything, it opens up everything.

WHEN YOU TRUST IN YOURSELF TO HANDLE *ANY*THING, IT EMBOLDENS YOU FOR *EVERY*THING. EMBRACE YOUR UNCERTAINTY.

Neuroscientists have found that our brains are wired to look for patterns. So when we're in an uncertain situation — a common occurrence in today's increasingly 'VUCA' (volatile, uncertain, complex, ambiguous) world, it triggers anxiety as our brains struggle to discern the best course of action. For instance, one experiment found that people were less anxious when they knew exactly when they were going to get an electric shock than they were when they didn't know whether one might be coming or not! As Archy de Berker from University

College London wrote, 'Knowing for sure that your plane is cancelled can be less stressful than being kept in nervous suspense as it is repeatedly delayed.'

FOCUSING ON WHAT YOU *DON'T* WANT CONSUMES ENERGY BETTER SPENT CREATING WHAT YOU *DO* WANT.

Wired as we are to control against uncertainty, the reality is that you cannot future proof against every potential outcome and mitigate against every potential risk. Far wiser is to do as Eckhart Tolle wrote in *The Power Of Now*: 'Surrender is to accept the present moment unconditionally and without reservation.' From this place you can respond far more powerfully to whatever comes next, free to adapt and respond and intervene or simply let go as life unfolds before you.

In fact, focusing on what lays ahead can just fuel anxiety, impairing our ability to think clearly and deal with what's in front of us right now. Research by David Rock of the NeuroLeadership Institute found an inverse relationship between our anxiety levels and our cognition levels. When we're stressed, we're more likely to stare blankly at a computer screen rather than focus on the task at hand. As Rock wrote, 'People are more likely to solve problems with insight if they are in a positive mood.'

Rock's words brings to mind the famous quote by Mark Twain who said that he had known many troubles in his life, most of which never happened. Anxiety about what might — *or might never* — happen in your future makes you less equipped to handle whatever ends up happening. Rather, focus on the moment right in front of you and keep faith that you will rise to the challenges of every other moment as it arises. In short, live your worry once.

So let me ask you, if you were to embrace your struggles as part and parcel of your human experience, how would that lighten the mental load you're carrying?

When your anxiety-meter starts dialling up, you start turning your forecasts into 'fear-casts'. Fear-casting is less about predicting the future and more about conjuring up dark threatening futures to scare ourselves back into the cave. The more easily we can imagine a negative event happening, the more we tend to overestimate the likelihood that it will. Hence why people get so scared about dying in a plane crash, which is statistically very unlikely. In truth, you're more likely to die of the common flu.

BEWARE OF 'FEAR-CASTING': TERRORISING YOURSELF WITH WORST-CASE SCENARIOS THAT ROB YOU OF YOUR PRESENT AND CONSTRICT YOUR ACTIONS TO IMPROVE YOUR FUTURE.

Researchers have found that a central feature of anxiety is people's thoughts about threat and danger that leave them seeing big problems in small things. Anxiety-prone people tend towards 'what next' beliefs where they are constantly scanning their environment for all the catastrophes and dangers that could be lurking around the next corner. As psychologist Dr Ellen Hendriksen wrote, 'This is the dubious talent of anxiety — the ability to take a situation that's anywhere from ambiguous to slightly threatening, and forecast a really big catastrophe.' Since our emotions are contagious by nature, the more often we dwell on things that make us anxious, the more anxious we become.

So if you're feeling at all anxious right now, ask yourself this:

How bad could it really be and how likely is it to happen?

What if, instead of conjuring up those worst-case scenarios in a futile effort to future-proof yourself against disappointment, you replaced *uncertainty* with *possibility* and opened your arms wide to all the amazing things that could happen for you? After all, the less energy you spend stressing over all the 'what if' or 'what next' scenarios, the more you have to create the best possible 'what could be' outcomes.

Embracing uncertainty doesn't mean giving up trying to improve your future. Nor is it about passively sitting back and going with the flow. Far from it. Rather it's about being an active participant in making the very best of the situation you're currently in while working to improve it. For me, this means making the most of living in Singapore while working on options to get my family all back on the same continent (and who knows, by the time you're reading this book, we might be).

In the end, it all boils down to the lens through which you choose to frame your life. As the poet Francis J. Allison wrote:

> *A crowd of troubles passed him by*
>
> *As he with courage waited;*
>
> *He said, 'Where do your troubles fly*
>
> *When you are thus belated?'*
>
> *'We go,' they say, 'to those who mope,*
>
> *Who look on life dejected,*
>
> *Who meekly say "goodbye" to hope,*
>
> *We go where we're expected.'*

So expect good things to happen. Not just when you feel like you've got everything under control, but even more so when you know you haven't. Those storms you thought were ruining your plans and disrupting your path may actually just be revealing it.

LIFE'S STORM MAY BE UNWANTED AND FEEL UNFAIR. BUT CONSIDER THAT RATHER THAN DISRUPTING YOUR PATH, THEY'RE ACTUALLY REVEALING IT.

Maybe right now actively pursuing an uncertain path is the last thing on your mind. Perhaps what you most need at this moment in time is to let go of your resistance and say yes to the uncertainty of the path you're on!

There are points in our lives when simply showing up for life is a mental triumph. I've known a few — those days where it's about simply keeping your head above water, one hour at a time. Sometimes, when our world has been tilted on its axis, showing up and standing upright is *all* life asks of us.

In which case, go on ... say 'Yes!'

Say yes to life as it is.

Say *yes* to yourself *as you are*.

And say yes to the trust you will place in yourself that whatever unfolds ahead, you can handle it and you have the capacity to weather any storm.

YOU ARE THE LIGHT THAT YOU SEEK.
YOU HOLD THE CERTAINTY YOU WISH FOR.
WHENEVER YOU FEEL LOST, LOOK WITHIN.

As for me, I have no idea what my future holds, but I do know this … when nothing is certain, everything is possible.

In the words of Elizabeth Lesser, co-founder of health and wellness retreat, Omega Institute, 'This is my prayer to God everyday. Remove the veils here so that I may not be intoxicated by my worries and my fears.'

'Our role in life
is to bring the light
of our own souls
to the dim places
around us.'

Joan Chittister

12

Own Your Power

Lead the change you want to see

It had been a long few days for Linda Cruse. As she made the long drive back to her home outside London from a sales conference in the north of England, she was tired, bone tired. Not that working long hours were anything new to her. She'd worked long hours for years. She also drank too much, slept too little and felt trapped in her job with no way out.

Suddenly, without any warning, everything went dark. She could see nothing, absolutely nothing. Somehow she managed to pull her car over to the side of the motorway, a feat she later recalled as a small miracle in itself. And there she sat, totally blind, imprisoned by a black void.

In those moments of utter darkness, time stood still and her years ahead flashed before her. What use would she be blind, unable to see ... unable to continue in her high-paying sales job. She was a single mother with two children depending on her. Despair washed over her. Then terror. She hadn't prayed for years, but in that darkest of moments, she surrendered her doubts to the possibility of a higher force. 'God, if you will give me back my eyesight, I promise that I will find the reason I was born to live and I will live it.'

Linda spent months recovering. The doctors said her temporary blindness had been brought on by prolonged chronic stress and acute exhaustion. But that moment of blindness ignited a spark within her. Once fully well, she took a huge leap of faith to start a new life as an international humanitarian. Drawing on her training as a nurse and commercial skills in sales, she was committed to being wherever she could be of greatest service and harnessing the ingenuity of people in the corporate world to solve the most pressing humanitarian problems.

Several years later, Linda woke up one morning to the news that a giant tsunami had hit the coasts of Thailand, Indonesia and Sri Lanka. She knew at once where she had to be. Two days later, Linda walked out of an airport in southern Thailand into the warm tropical air and caught a taxi that would take her to a survivors camp where 5000 people in desperate need were being housed. As the car reached the coastline, her mind could hardly comprehend what her eyes were witnessing. Bodies, hundreds of them, floating lifeless in the water. The scale of death and devastation was unlike anything she'd seen before, and she'd seen a lot.

She asked the driver to pull over and got out of the car. She walked over to the side of a nearby cliff and sat down, overwhelmed by the enormity of the suffering she was headed towards. She just felt she could not go on, that she would have to return to the airport. It was all too much. And then she was struck by a vision. She flashed back to herself at eighteen, in nurse training, standing in front of her nurse matron. 'It's not about you,' her matron said. 'It's about what you're here to do.'

We all arrive at moments in our life where we are tested. Do we heed the call to advance amid our uncertainty and misgivings, or do we retreat to the familiarity of the known — to where little is required from us and our comfort feels assured?

In an age when David is easily reduced to a comic figure and Goliath the norm, we will always find reasons to justify retreat, to cast ourselves as powerless against the larger forces around us and settle where we are, no matter how dry the nest or deep our yearning for more.

Who am I to be so bold, so audacious, so daring?

I'm so insignificant against the enormity of the challenge.

So ill-equipped for the size of the endeavour.

What good can I do? What mark can I make?

And who am I to think I can do any at all?

So much could go wrong. So much I put at risk.

Ah yes, but what do you put at risk if you don't?

It is part of the human condition to live our lives with an internal tug of war, regularly torn between conflicting desires, trading-off between needs at cross-purposes with each other.

Comfort versus growth.

Looking good versus doing good.

Familiarity versus adventure.

Social approval versus authentic self-expression.

Immediate pleasure versus long-term fulfilment.

Appeasing our desire for admiration, approval and accolades will always be in tension with our highest aspirations for contribution, connection and enlightenment.

And so we are all faced with a daily (sometimes hourly) choice:

Which side of this internal tug of war will we pull behind?

Our small self is clear where it stands — play it safe, protect our pride, avoid risking the comforts we have now for the lure of what we'd love most. So we must be equally relentless in plugging into the noblest part of our being, the part from which we access our deepest source of strength to reach for our highest aspirations.

It's why when it all boils down to it, living your best life requires living a brave life. Being prepared to lay your pride, your fear and your vulnerability on the line for the sake of a nobler clause.

Your highest truth. Your deepest values. Your greatest legacy.

LEADING CHANGE, IN YOUR LIFE AND THE WORLD, WILL ALWAYS REQUIRE LAYING YOUR PRIDE ON THE LINE FOR THE SAKE OF A NOBLER CAUSE.

Which brings me to the most compelling question that you must ask yourself, again and again and again:

What do you want your life to stand for?

If you do not stand firmly for values that align with the highest vision for your life and honour the good you can do, you will, by default, err down the path of greatest short-term comfort and minimal inconvenience. Stand for nothing, fall for anything.

'The great use of a life is to spend it for something that will outlast it,' wrote William James. Examine the lives of the most exceptional human beings throughout history, and a common theme will emerge. They were not driven by a desire to accumulate power for their own sake; they were driven to use the power they had for the sake of a grander vision, one that would outlast them.

That exact same power resides in you.

Each time you don't trust in your power, you weaken your connection to it.

Each time you do trust in it, you do just the opposite. You amplify it.

Think of power like an electric current. You cannot see it. You might never understand it. Yet the invisibility and mystery of this force doesn't negate its power. Likewise, just because you don't always feel powerful doesn't mean you have no power. It simply means, like a lamp that is not plugged in to the electric socket, you're not connected into it.

Few people have written about the power that resides within each of us more poignantly than my friend Marianne Williamson did in her book *A Return to Love*:

> *Our greatest fear is not that we are inadequate, but that we are powerful beyond measure. It is our light, not our darkness, that frightens us. We ask ourselves, Who am I to be brilliant, gorgeous, handsome, talented and fabulous? Actually, who are you not to be? You are a child of God. Your playing small does not serve the world. There is nothing enlightened about shrinking so that other people won't feel insecure around you. We were born to make manifest the glory of God within us. It is not just in some; it is in everyone. And, as we let our own light shine, we consciously give other people permission to do the same. As we are liberated from our fear, our presence automatically liberates others.*

We are living in turbulent times. There are people in our midst who are using their power to incite fear, to fuel division, and to undermine our trust in ourselves and each other. Which is why it is so important that we each use the power within us to be ambassadors for the world we want to create together — that we show the leadership we yearn for in those charged to lead us.

US President Abraham Lincoln once wrote:

The dogmas of the quiet past are inadequate to the stormy present. The occasion is piled high with difficulty and we must rise with the occasion. As our case is new, we must think anew and act anew.

Lincoln led the US through the bloodiest chapter of its history. Yet his words are no less relevant in today's 'stormy times', which apply not just to one country, or culture, but to our world.

STEP INTO YOUR POWER TO BECOME AN AMBASSADOR FOR THE WORLD YOU WANT TO LIVE IN.

In stormy times we are each called to step up — individually, collectively, powerfully. As leadership authority Margaret Wheatley says, 'I cannot imagine a more important task in this time than to consciously choose who we want to be as a leader.'

As I travel around the world to speak about leading with courage, I often meet people who shy from the suggestion of being a 'leader'.

I'm not a leader. I've never had a title. I don't manage people. I wouldn't know how.

If the word 'leader' doesn't sit with you, fine. Pick another. But consider the possibility that your ideas of what a leader looks like or what it takes to be a leader are confining you, cutting you off from doing the one thing you could do today that would make the most meaningful difference to yourself and others.

The truth is that every single one of us — regardless of our past, our position, or formal power — has an opportunity to show leadership. We do this each time we consciously decide to be a positive force for change in whatever capacity we have. The only thing keeping anyone from being a leader in their own workplace, community and life, is the courage to step up to the plate and act as one.

And one of the most powerful ways we can grow our capacity for effecting positive change is through how we speak: harnessing our words to change our world, beginning with speaking differently about the inner landscape of our lives.

AT THE HEART OF LEADERSHIP IS THE COURAGE TO ACT AS ONE.

SPEAK POWERFULLY

The words you speak hold immense power — power to open up possibilities or close them down; power to build trust or division; power to inspire brave action or fuel fear, anger, blame or self-pity.

Your subconscious interprets what it hears literally. Where your words lead, your emotions and body will follow. The language you use not only shapes how powerful you feel in yourself but how others perceive you as well.

When you use positive, forward-leaning language about yourself and your ability to meet your challenges, then that is what tends to show up for you externally. Likewise, if you continually make declarations that echo hopelessness and nurture anxiety, pessimism and powerlessness, then that will also shape your reality.

As ingrained as our linguistic habits can become, it's entirely within your power to use new language that will fuel your self-belief and affirm your resolve to rise above your challenges and to make the changes you've been putting off.

So stand tall in your power, embody confidence, and speak in ways that reflect the person who you want to become — using language that is positive, powerful and purposeful. Here are seven ways to use the power of language to lead change from the inside out:

1. **Frame forward.** Instead of expressing yourself in terms of what you cannot do, reframe your language in ways that express what you *can* do and the actions you *will* take to improve your situation, e.g. instead of *I can't, I don't, I won't, I wish,* say *I can, I am, I will, I choose, I have, I create* ...

2. **Mind absolutes**. Using absolute language in a negative context cuts you off from influencing positive outcomes. So avoid over-generalising and restate things in ways that open new doors to action, not close them down.

    'This situation is impossible' becomes 'this is a challenging situation'.

    'I'm never going to solve this problem' becomes 'I've yet to figure it out ... *yet!*'

    'I'm always hopeless at ...' becomes 'I'm learning how to ...'

3. **Avoid melodrama.** 'It's such a nightmare', 'It's killing me', 'I'll just die if ...', 'It's a total catastrophe', 'I'm destroyed ...' Your words create your reality. So avoid language that talks up stress and fuels drama rather than fuelling your confidence to meet your challenges.

4. **Limit labels.** When used on pantry jars, labels are helpful. Yet used on situations and people, they can reinforce an undesired state and hem you in by subconsciously encouraging you to conform to them. For instance, labelling yourself into a certain role (e.g. 'I'm just a housewife, assistant ...') constrains your brain from even considering how you could be anything more. Labelling yourself by your weaknesses does the same. For example, instead of 'I'm disorganised' say 'I'm working on being more organised.' Same for how you explain events. Instead of 'I'm a failure' say 'I didn't succeed at *that* task on *that* occasion.' Remember, failure is an event, not a person.

5. **Speak possibilities.** Orville and Wilbur Wright didn't get an aircraft off the ground by focusing on what had never been done, but by challenging the boundaries of what could. If you want to achieve something new, talk about how it excites you and what you'll do to bring it into reality, not on arguing for all the reasons 'why not'. For instance, if you want more influence, talk about how you'll use the influence you already have.

6. **Express resolve.** President John F. Kennedy didn't say 'let's try to get a man on the moon'. He said 'By the end of this decade we *will* get a man on the moon.' Using committed language that echoes a 'can-do' spirit shifts the energy you bring to your challenges and rallies support from others in ways that 'trying', 'wishing' and 'hoping for the best' never will. For instance, saying 'I am a leader' (or entrepreneur or activist) is your first step to becoming one.

7. **Rephrase problems into opportunities.** Einstein once said that problems cannot be solved at the same level of thinking at which they were created. When you shift your language around your problems, it shifts your energy around them. New ideas and opportunities will unfold accordingly. 'It's really hard' becomes 'It's an opportunity for growth'; 'I'm nervous' becomes 'I'm excited.' Reframing your biggest problem into the opportunity it holds is the first step to solving it.

Waiting for those who have been appointed to positions of formal power to fix the biggest problems you face in your world — in *our* world — is naive, even dangerous. We must be proactive participants in shaping the future we want to live in. This requires each of us to step into our own power — as leaders, change makers, power brokers, activists and advocates — beginning with what we're called to change within our own lives and extending outward. Complacency only makes us complicit in the very things we rail against.

EVERY TIME YOU TAKE ACTION AMID YOUR FEAR, YOU DILUTE ITS POWER AND AMPLIFY YOUR OWN.

Daring to think of yourself as someone with power will amplify your power. This isn't just fluffy thinking, it's been validated in scans of our brains circuitry. As a study by Professor Herminia Ibarra of London Business School found, when we start to act as though we are a leader — regardless of our position or title or any formal leadership authority we might have — over time we begin to think as a leader and to be seen as a leader. It becomes a self-reinforcing loop. And it begins with one single decision. To trust in yourself, in your innate capacity to effect change, and to take action. Courageous action.

Which begs the question, where is courage calling you to step up in a bigger way?

To dial up your daring and pursue the boldest vision for your life.

To defy your doubts and risk the failure you fear.

To do more of what strengthens you and less of what doesn't.

To trust your gifts and heed that tug on your heart.

To embrace your vulnerability and express your truth.

To lower your mask and lean on those who lift you up.

Author Yung Pueblo wrote that 'True power is living the realisation that you are your own healer, hero, leader.' No matter what your situation right now — however daunting your challenges, bold your ambitions, or overwhelming your doubts — take a big deep breath and trust that you hold the key to the power you long for.

No-one else.

Just you.

In her book *The Moment of Lift*, Melinda Gates wrote that, 'Working on ourselves while working to help others is the inner and outer work — where the effort to change the world and the effort to change ourselves come together.' It's true. Our ability to improve the world around us is fully dependent on our commitment to improve the world within us. This is big work. It's our life's work. As fourteenth-century Christian mystic Meister Eckhart wrote, 'The outer work can never be small if the inner work is great. And the outer work can never be great if the inner work is small.'

VISUALISE YOURSELF AS A LEADER, A CHANGE-MAKER, A FORCE FOR GOOD — AND THEN SHOW UP AS ONE.

Just imagine the world we could create together if each of us were to connect to the deepest truth within us and step toward higher ground, rooted in our innate sufficiency. Just imagine how it would transform our governments and corporations and schools and communities and homes and war zones if, instead of working to cover up our deep sense of insecurity, insufficiency and inferiority we could own these emotions while leaning into our faith that we are innately whole, already 'enough' and an invaluable member of the whole human family.

I am only one, but still I am one,

I cannot do everything.

But still I can do something;

And because I cannot do everything

I will not refuse to do the something that I can do.

When you commit to doing that which you can do, however meagre it feels, you can make a unique imprint on this world, one unlike that of anyone who has come before you or will come after you. As history has shown time and time again, one person committed to changing the world has more power than a million who aren't. Remember the young man in front of that tank in Tiananmen Square? Or Greta Thunberg in front of the UN Assembly?

In his book *Power vs Force*, David Hawkins wrote that 'We are each accountable to the universe.' One distant day, many years from now, we will have to reconcile ourselves with the choices we made and the lives we lived ... including the unlived lives we *didn't live*, the gifts we *didn't share*, the people we *didn't lift*.

Which begs the question:

If you stay your current course, what might you one day regret?

You cannot go back and make a brand-new start in your life. But your past does not dictate your future. You do. And so every day you have the chance to begin it anew. To reset your sights on the boldest vision for your life — one that aligns with the call to courage of your highest self. In which case, what vision inspires you? What pursuits would bring new life to your living and purpose into your days?

I cannot know your answer to that question. But I do know this: it lives inside you. And if you're being really honest with yourself, you also know that as uncomfortable as change can be, in the long arc of life, it will leave you in a far more comfortable place than spending it wondering who you might have been, what you might have done, had only you trusted yourself and dared to believe in the potential left dormant within.

Of course, no-one is brave all the time. But many times life calls us to be braver than we want to be. So on the days you fall short and your small self has notched up a few wins, be kind to yourself and commit to doing better tomorrow. Even if just a little bit.

Because here's what I know for sure. Everything you need to leave your imprint on the world, and on the hearts of those you share yours with, lies within you.

Everything.

You don't need a title or an MBA. You don't need a wealthy backer or a power network of 'influencers'. (Such things can help of course, but they are not a prerequisite.) You just need to trust that as you move towards what lights you up, your sense of your own power will magnify. Because in the end, the biggest barrier keeping you from showing up as a truly powerful person is your unwillingness to trust in the power that already resides within you.

> WITHIN YOU IS A PLACE THAT IS FREE OF INSECURITIES, HURTS FROM YOUR PAST OR FEARS FOR YOUR FUTURE. IT IS THE SOURCE OF YOUR REAL POWER — YOUR TRUE SELF — AND IT'S HERE FOR YOU RIGHT NOW.

Several months before to embarking on this book, I caught up Marianne Williamson during a trip to New York. Sitting in her apartment, I asked her what projects she was working on.

'I'm thinking of running for president,' she replied. I must admit, it was not the response I'd been expecting. But then, Marianne is not one for trivial pursuits.

A few months later, Marianne announced her candidacy for the Democratic nomination for the 2020 US presidential campaign. She entered the combative arena of presidential politics knowing full well that it would expose her to personal attacks and scorching criticism. She was fully aware of the challenge she'd face to secure the poll numbers and funds amid a crowded field of far better-known career politicians. Yet, as she shared with me midway through her campaign as I neared the end of this book, during another visit to New York,

> *I love this country too much not to give my very best to address the deeper causes underlying the problems America is facing. After all, democracy is not just about our rights, it's about our responsibilities.*

Mentioning Marianne has nothing to do with partisanship or political power. It has *everything* to do with personal power.

Your personal power. My personal power. Our collective power.

Leading change is not the work of the few; it is the work of the many. We all have the power to influence change. When we fail to use the power that lies within our control, we surrender it for others to wield it for us. It is the small choices we make to use our power — day in, day out — that expand our power, and shift the trajectory of our lives and the state of our hearts. This is as true at the individual level as at the collective level.

WHEN WE DON'T USE THE POWER WITHIN OUR CONTROL, WE SURRENDER THAT POWER FOR OTHERS TO WIELD FOR US.

When I was living in Virginia, another friend, Caren Merrick, decided to run for the state congress. In the lead-up to election day, Caren knocked on 10 000 doors and, like Marianne, campaigned against the odds in a district whose electoral boundaries were stacked against her. In the end, she failed to win. Yet her voice was heard and her time was not wasted. After all, to circle back to Roosevelt, 'Working hard at work worth doing' is never time wasted.

Caren sat on the opposite side of the political aisle as Marianne. I cheered for them both because not only do my friendships transcend political allegiances and ideologies, but because I believe the best solutions don't come from one side of the fence or another. Rather they emerge from the debate that occurs when people who have a heart for others come together to find a better path forward. This can only occur when more decent people steeped in values, integrity, civility and empathy dare to enter into the arena — political and otherwise. As my dear friend Ron Kaufman says, 'We must put the heart of others at the heart of all we do.'

So as you near the final page of this book and prepare to get on with the rest of your life, I encourage you to clarify the values you want to put at the heart of your life.

Kindness. Community. Compassion. Faith. Family. Service. Creativity. Sustainability. Peace. Love. Potential. Leadership. Adventure. Justice. Forgiveness. Inclusion. Humour. Hope. Beauty. Self-expression. Learning. Gratitude. Equality. Generosity. Environment. Exploration. Reconciliation. Spirituality.

Nelson Mandela wrote, 'There is no passion to be found in playing small, in settling for a life that is less than the life you are capable of living.'

WE ARE EACH ON OUR OWN HERO'S JOURNEY OF BECOMING — OF PEELING BACK THE VEILS OF FEAR AND FALSEHOOD THAT HAVE LEFT US A STRANGER TO THE MAGNIFICENCE OF WHO WE ARE.

Of course, many times in the years ahead you'll fall short of living up to your values as the tug of your small self gets the better of you. Literally. Such is what it is to be human. To fall short, and fall down, and fail to live up to our noblest intentions.

We are all in this human bandwagon together; all doing our best to navigate the 'whole catastrophe' of life's roller coaster adventure ride together. And while some appear to be riding the crest of an eternal wave, almost immune to life's storms, none of us ever truly arrive. We are always in the process of becoming.

Or, depending on how you frame the human experience, of unbecoming. As Brazilian novelist Paulo Coelho wrote,

> *Maybe the journey isn't so much about becoming anything. Maybe it's about un-becoming everything that isn't really you, so you can be who you were meant to be in the first place.*

Who you were 'meant to be in the first place' isn't about being more like anyone else. Nor is it about becoming a Nobel Laureate or Branson protégé. It *is* about deliberately and repeatedly choosing to back the biggest part of yourself, pursuing a vision for your life that eclipses your fear.

And on those occasions when your fears win the arm wrestle, to forgive your fallibility, keep faith and press forward.

If life were perfect, it wouldn't be.

If you were perfect, you wouldn't be.

It is in the imperfection of your life today, right now — for all that is just as you'd like it to be and for all that is not remotely close to ideal — in which lies the richest opportunities for you to grow, to learn, and to blossom into the wholeness of the person you could never otherwise become.

Two roads diverged in a wood, and I—

I took the one less traveled by,

And that has made all the difference.

Sometimes these paths Robert Frost wrote about will come in the form of life-changing decisions. Other times, the choices will seem less consequential. Do not underestimate the cumulative impact of seemingly small decisions and insignificant actions across the totality of your life.

To stop making excuses and take full ownership for what's not working.

To embrace discomfort, lean into vulnerability and put yourself 'out there'.

To trust your talents, defy your doubts and take charge of your future.

Most of all, to place faith in yourself that no matter what happens on your adventures ahead ...

You've got this!

IF YOU TRULY TRUSTED IN YOUR POWER TO LIVE
THE BOLDEST VISION FOR YOUR LIFE, WHAT
WOULD YOU DO? GO ON, DARE YOURSELF,
TRUST YOURSELF, ASTONISH YOURSELF.

Einstein once said that there are only two ways to live our lives — either as though nothing is a miracle or everything is a miracle. Yet choosing to live your life as a miracle is not a choice you make just once. It's a choice you will be called on to make again and again and again. To trust in the miracle that brought you into existence to begin with. To trust in the miracle that somehow landed this book into your hands. To trust in the miracle of every experience in your life right now and how every single one of them has brought you to this place you are at today, knowing what you know, feeling what you feel, certain about yourself in a way you may not have felt before.

And yet *still* learning, and *still* discovering and *still* uncovering and *still* pulling back the veils that have kept you from yourself.

In Joseph Campbell's 'the hero's journey', the protagonist arrives back where he began.

We're all walking our own hero's journey; and each day we wake up we have the opportunity to start anew in building the self-trust heroism requires.

Brick by brick, day by day, one brave act of heroism at a time, you build the self-trust that lays at the foundation of living a life that matters; one that elevates you and all around you.

You do it each time, to circle back to where this book began: you choose to act braver than you want to be. You do it each time you decide not to wait until all doubt is gone before you take a wild leap towards the highest and holiest vision for your life. Most of all, you do it each time you trust that within you lays the light that you seek — to grow into the greatness of the person you've always sensed, in the quiet hidden depths, that you were born to become.

What if you fall?

Ah yes, but what if you fly?

Your wings are stronger than you know.

Your heart more powerful than you can imagine.

Trust in your wings, honour your gifts, believe in the beauty of your dreams.

I began this book by saying that even if I could dissolve your doubts or remove your fears (which I cannot), it would not serve you anyway. That's because it is who you will become by learning to transcend your fears and embrace the full spectrum of your humanity that will ultimately complete your hero's journey.

So can I trust you to say yes to one final request?

But of course, you say.

It's this.

That each day (or as often as you can manage), you recommit to living your one and only precious life as the miracle it is, grounded in faith, and trusting yourself that

You've Got This!

Because, if there is one message that my heart is called to imprint upon your own, it's that you have.

You've Got This!
Manifesto

You are exactly where you're intended to be
and possess all that's required to meet the demands of this day.

Who you are is not your hurts from the past or fears for the future.
Not your doubts or struggles or the stories you've spun that have kept
you from rising strong or daring to pursue your boldest aspirations.

Right now, at this moment, your one task above all others is this:

TRUST IN YOURSELF

Trust that the power within you transcends all problems outside you.
Trust that you are innately worthy, wholly adequate and
uniquely gifted for what tugs most at your heart.
Trust the quiet whispers urging you toward the braver path,
toward the highest vision and noblest purpose,
for your one and only sacred life.

Every day of your journey has prepared you for this one.

So embrace your fears and fallibility. Embrace your hardships and heartaches.
Embrace your unanswered questions, your impatience and uncertainty for what's ahead.

Each hold a silent invitation to peel back the layers keeping you a stranger to yourself,
so that you may discover the depths of your true power and honour
the brilliance of your potential still lying dormant within.

The light you seek is within you. It requires only your trust.
When you doubt yourself you dim that light
and short change the world.

Breathe in faith. Breathe out fear.
Breathe in faith again.

YOU'VE GOT THIS

Always.

ACKNOWLEDGEMENTS

The writing of this book took place over a period in my life that I know I'll one day look back upon as one of immense uncertainty, family disruption and personal growth. As I write now, in the final days before this book goes off for typesetting, the future is still uncertain. So I am more present than ever to the people in my life who've supported me throughout this period.

My first acknowledgement needs to go to Lucy Raymond, Bronwyn Evans, Ingrid Bond, my editor Allison Hiew, and all the team at Wiley, in Australia, Asia and the USA, for their support of a book that not only went well over the original word scope, but outside the lines of the traditional business genre. Thank you for entrusting me to write a book on trusting oneself. In the spirit of dialling up my own daring, I hope this book will vindicate your trust, emboldening millions to choose the path of faith over fear and take braver actions that build stronger outcomes — in every domain of work, leadership, love and life.

A deeply heartfelt thank you also to my many dear and treasured friends covering many time zones around the world for the countless times you've expressed your faith in me. The title of this book was originally inspired by the refrain I've said to others thousands of times, but it's also one I've valued hearing just as many. The big-hearted people who make up my global tribe are too numerous to list, but I feel compelled to list the names of a good few: *Anna, Maryellen, Susan, Sarah, Lizzy, Jane, Nic, Nadine, Ron, Mary, Gaby, Steve, Cindy, Chris, Jacinta, Dalia, Sonia, Fletch, Denise, Becky, Farina, Lynn, Debra, Julie, Joan, Tamera, Godelieve, Christine, Amanda, Joanna, Suzi, Michelle, Gina, Will, Malcom, Susie, Paul and Kelly.* In different ways, you've given me the uplift I've needed on days when my monkey mind was racing anxious laps of *what ifs.*

A special shout out to my assistant Angela. I wouldn't dare take on half as much as I do without your constant support and thinking two steps ahead of me. You're not only a superb right-hand woman, you are a true friend.

To my mum and dad, thank you for giving me deep roots, strong wings and an appreciation of what makes for a truly rich life. To Frank, Pauline, Steve, Anne, Cath and all in the extended Kleinitz clan, you're all gold in my life.

Finally, my own family. Andrew, your deep faith in me over the last 28 years has emboldened me to rise above my doubts and grow into the woman I am today. While the last few years have been fraught with disruption and uncertainty, your integrity to your values has never wavered. I'm not only proud of you, but I admire your dedication to growing into the compassionate leader you feel called to be in the world. I know we'll both emerge the other side of this period more grounded, humble and whole-hearted than we were before, though I suspect not much more patient. Sharing life's wondrous and wild ride by your side is one of my life's greatest blessings, even the bumpy bits.

Lachlan, as your faith has deepened, it's increasingly bolstered my own. I could not be more proud of you and more in awe of your compassion for those who suffer on society's sidelines. You know *you've got this* because you are so clear of the 'Way Maker' who has you. What a privilege to be your mum.

Feisty, feminine, fabulous and funny — Maddy, you are all these things and so many *many* more. I hope this book will remind you of what I've so often told you ... that you're uniquely talented and have everything it takes to blaze a life that lights you up and lifts up so many others. Just trust in your brilliance, and be patient as the world catches up!

Ben, you've rolled with the punches and handled the disruption of these last few years with the same good-humoured temperament you've had since you moved countries as an eight-week-old! Thank you for lightening our load at every turn with your effervescence and upbeat 'she'll be right' outlook (not to mention for being such a great sport about being the last to leave home!). Your personality is infectious and I'm excited by the mark you'll make in the years ahead.

Matt — four high schools, with three curriculums, across three continents, within sixteen months ... that's rough in anyone's books. Yet as hard as some weeks were, you stepped up and proved your mettle. You came out of the womb ready to take on the world and while the last few years have challenged you, they've also moulded you into an incredibly impressive (and adaptable!) young leader with broad shoulders and a big heart that makes mine swell with pride.

Last of all, I must acknowledge the source that has grounded and emboldened my own self-trust time and time again. If Thomas Merton's words that 'anxiety is a sign of spiritual insecurity' hold truth, then I clearly still have work to do. Yet without my faith in a higher spiritual force at play in my life and our world, this book would not have found its way from my heart into your hands. If it's inspired you in walking your own path of faith over fear in any small way, I am deeply honoured. I'm also a humble testament to what I wrote in these pages — that we shouldn't waste our time putting in what God left out, but rather give our best to drawing out what God left in.

And last of all, an acknowledgement to you for bearing with me to the end. I hope you'll return to these pages again in the years ahead and that each time you do, you'll read something that lifts you up, lightens your load and reaffirms the voice of your true self — that the power within you transcends any problem outside you, because ... yes, you know I've got to say it ... *You've Got This!*

Love and Light,

Margie x

INDEX

Throughout the index 'MW' stands for the author, Margie Warrell

accountability 198

'act as if' 10

action, taking 3–17, 53
— Brenda's story 11–12, 51
— importance of 12–13, 48–49
— Lyn Kraus's story 13–14

adversity 88, 161, 176
— and resistance 174–175

affect, positive 62

affirmation, power of 30–32
— steps in 31–32
— suggestions for 33

ambition 38–44, 111, 113
— negative associations 41–44
— what you can give 42–43

amplification 118–119, 196–197, 199–200

anxiety 10, 26–27, 45–46, 48, 68, 100–101, 142, 143, 148, 168, 169, 183–185, 194

appreciation 70–71, 101–102

aspirations 46, 111

assumptive world 175

Batty, Rosie 180–181

beating yourself up 62–63, 65–66, 68, 69

beauty, dealing with 119–120

beginning before you feel ready 3–17

behaviours
— changing 10–11
— theories of 21

beliefs see also faith
— false 12
— useful 30

best, giving your 104–105

best life 191
— small self 21

bias against women 108

blame 26, 62, 66, 98–99, 111–112, 167–168, 175

book club story 159–160

'boys will be boys' 128
brain 15, 24; *see also*
   neuropsychology
— neuroplasticity 67–68
— pathways 67–68
— processing information 31
Branson, Richard 14, 44, 93, 158,
   201
brave life, 190, 191–192
Brenda's story 8–9, 11–12
Brown, Shivaun 29–30
Brown, Tania 100

capacity for life 86
career development, MW's 47–50,
   178–179
— life coaching 49, 146, 155–157
— writing 102–103, 155–157,
   173
CB radio and technology 91–92
challenges
— accepting 190–192
— overcoming *see* men,
   overcoming challenges;
   women, overcoming
   challenges
— sharing 64
change *see also* power, owning your
   own; resistance,
   surrendering
— embracing 179–181, 198
— leading 189–193, 200
— resisting 177–178
Chinese handcuffs story 176
choices 4–5
comfort 25

— growth and 7, 8, 10, 11–12,
   45–46, 52–53, 134, 177, 183,
   191–192
— zone 45, 158, 166
comparisons, danger of making
   51–52
compassion 74, 169, 180–181
competence 13
complaining 177
confidence *see also* affirmation,
   power of
— acting with 10–11
— effects of lack of 28
— four pillars of 19
— Milly's story 26–27, 30
— overrated 7
— undermining 26–27
— waiting for 3–17
confirmation bias 99
connecting 64–65; *see also* career
   development, MW's
— avoiding 27, 28
— book club story 159–160
— challenging 65–66
— co-operation, power of 154–
   155
— courage 162
— difficult 27
— doubters 168–169
— geese analogy 154, 157
— lifting others, value of 163–165
— Mt Kilimanjaro story 163–165
— negative responses 169
— openness 161–162
— people who provide uplift
   153–169

— power of 153–154
— redwoods story 162
— risk, taking 155–156
— sharing the struggle 160–161
— support, providing 155–157,
    165, 166, 167
— wired for 157
Cooper, Jacqui 22
co-operation, power of 154–155
courage 11, 46, 47, 162, 165,
    196–197
— 10 Commandments of 114–
    120
crucible experiences 128–131
Cruse, Linda 189–190
crying 127, 128

difference, embracing 115–116
doubt(s) 19–35, 156, 165; *see also*
    inner critic; negativity; self-
    doubt; Ten Commandments
    of Courage
— choices and 27–28
— cost of 16, 21, 25–26, 27–28,
    30, 46
— danger of 19–35
— dealing with 10, 21, 22–26,
    28–33, 34, 87, 93, 110, 158,
    161, 167–168, 196, 197, 202,
    203
— disputing 22
— faith and 145, 179, 189
— fear and 19–35
— internal discourse of 19–20,
    22, 34, 87, 105, 156, 166
— men and 123, 133

— Milly's story
    26–27, 30
doubters 110, 168–169

education, MW's 41, 47–50,
    110–111
embarrassing moments 57–60, 61
emotional contagion 154, 169, 185;
    see also emotion(s)
emotion(s) 10, 25, 70, 79, 81,
    86, 88, 98–99, 115, 124,
    154, 180, 194, 197; *see also*
    emotional contagion; fear(s);
    negativity
— dealing with 88, 182–183
— EQ 83, 168
— faith and 141–142
— improving 68, 88
— men and 125–127, 128, 130,
    132–133, 134–135
— negative 65–66, 142,
    148, 169
— normalised 23
— physical effects of 183
— positive 62, 142–143, 154
— resilience 66
— toxic 168
empowerment 31, 47, 82–83, 88,
    95, 110, 116
equal partners 109–110
ethics 176
exercise 77–78, 80–81, 85
expectations, others' 38, 39, 41–42,
    130–131
experiences, dealing with negative
    47, 50

faith
— benefits of 148–150
— heath and 141–142
— higher plan 145–147
— Kate's story 146–147
— lightness and darkness 143–145
— Peter's death 143–145
— power of 139–140
— present, focus on 150
— vs fear 148–151
Fairfax, Warwick 42, 130–131
fake news 23
fallibility 69
faith over fear 139–151; *see also* faith
fear(s) *see also* emotion(s); faith
— effect of action on 16
— of failure 54
— falsehoods and 19
— greatest 192–193
— nature of 46–47
— power and 192–193
— revealing 128
— rising above 12
feedback, dealing with negative 65–66
feminism 108
Fillinger, Tamera 159–160
forgiveness 71
Frank's story 91–92, 182
future self 53–54

Gallup company 93
geese analogy 154, 157
gender confidence gap 110–111

gender norms 112, 125–127
gifts, using your 86, 91–105
— appreciation 101–102
— best, giving your 104–105
— blame 98–99
— comparisons, avoiding 96–97
— cultivating 92–93
— downplaying 101–101
— Frank's tech story 91–92
— growth 101–102
— intentional, being 94–95
— Marianne Williamson's story 102–103
— outsourcing 93
— regrets 99
— saving instead of using 97–98
— strengths, owning your 103
— strengths, using 93, 94–95
— taking for granted 13–104
— Tania Brown's story 100
— weaknesses 93
giving up 175–177
goals 29, 42–43, 44, 45, 46, 63, 70, 103, 109, 165
gratitude 68, 70, 74, 80, 84, 85, 89, 115, 200
grief
— dealing with 144–145, 175, 180–181
— stages of 175
growth 11, 101–102
— post-traumatic 128–131

habits 84
— building 84–85
— changing 68, 70

— of success 80
— morning rituals 80–81
happiness 28, 45, 52, 83
help, asking for 116–117
hotel lockout story 57–60, 61
humanity, embracing your own 60,
        62, 64–65, 68, 69, 71, 126,
        130, 133, 139, 142, 148, 203
humility 102–103
humour 62, 64–65, 69

imposter syndrome 100–101
inner critic 60–61, 62–63; *see also*
        doubt(s), internal discourse;
        negativity
inner sage 88–89
inspiration 44
intentional, being 94–95
intuition 86

Johnston, Janet 156–157
journaling 62–63, 73, 80, 81, 84,
        85, 86–87, 88, 131, 144–145

Kate's story 146–147
Kraus, Lyn 13–14

leadership 176, 193–194, 200
leaky pipeline 114
Lee, Kai-Fu 129–130
lifting others, value of
        163–165
loneliness 155, 161
loss, processing 180–181
lovability 132, 146–147
love letters to self 88

#metoo movement 109
McDonell, Jacinta 158–159
McQuaid, Michelle 69, 94
Maddy's story 5–6
Marriott, Bill 7
mastery of life 155
Milly's story 26–27, 30
men, overcoming challenges 123–
        135
— boys will be boys 128
— crucible experiences 128–131
— crying 127, 128
— displacement and
        disempowerment, feelings of
        123
— emotions 125–127, 128, 130,
        132–133, 134–135
— gender norms 125–127
— lovability 132
— maturity 129
— 'real man', ideas about 124–125
— strengths, using 130–132
— toxic masculinity 125–127,
        128
— uncertainty 133
— vulnerability 123, 126–129,
        132, 134
— weakness 128–129
meditation, mirror 66–67
mindfulness 66–67
mistakes, dealing with 72
motherhood and career
        113–114
mothers 6–7; *see also* parenting
Mt Kilimanjaro story
        163–165

Nashville conference story 57–60, 61

negativity 19, 65–66, 105, 142, 148, 169
— loops, short-circuiting 68

negativity bias 67

neuropsychology 15, 67

neuroscience and uncertainty 183–184

nice, being 114–115

no, saying 111

North Korean radios 19

Obama, Michelle 119–120

objectivity 88

opportunities, seeking 117

opportunity cost 27–28

overthinking 16

overwhelm, feeling of 81–82, 86

parents, MW's 37–40, 97

parents and parenting 6–7, 64, 128, 146; see also motherhood and career; mothers
— expectations 130–131

Peter, death of 143–145, 153

Pomerantz, Suzi 166

positive psychology 7

post-traumatic growth 128–131

power, owning your own 189–203
— accepting challenges 190–192
— accountability 198
— amplifying 196–197, 199–200
— brave life, 190, 191–192
— change, leading 189–193, 200
— courage 196–197

— fear 192–193
— improving the world 197–199
— influence of your past 198–199
— Linda Cruse's story 189–190
— vision and values 191–192, 200–201
— words, power of 193–195

problems, persistence of 175–176

reframing 9

regret 27, 60, 99

resilience 67

resistance, surrendering 171–187
— adversity 174–175
— anxiety 184–185
— change, embracing 179–181
— change, resisting 177–178
— Chinese handcuffs story 176
— complaining 177
— easy vs right 176
— Frank's story 182
— giving up the fight 175–177
— grief, dealing with 175, 180–181
— pain, dealing with 182
— persistence of a problem 175–176
— reframing the problem 171–174
— Rosie Batty's story 180–181
— uncertainty 183–186

risk 25–26
— embracing 8, 17
— taking 14, 27, 149

robbery in Papua New Guinea 47

role models 10–11

Roosevelt, Teddy 42, 200

safe, staying 44; *see also* comfort
saving instead of using 97–98
self
— future 53–54
— small 21–23, 24, 28, 191
— small defined 21
— small vs true 21–23, 24
— true defined 21–22
Self-Affirmation Theory 31
self-audit 24–25
self-belief 112
self-compassion 65, 73, 74
self-confidence *see* confidence
self-criticism 107–109
self-deprecation 115, 102–103
self-doubt 16, 19, 22, 23–24, 46,
      119, 155; *see also* doubt(s);
      Ten Commandments of
      Courage
— conquering 21, 22
— purpose of 20–21
— women 107, 108, 110, 114
self-forgiveness 71, 72–73
self-fullness 79–80
self-honesty 73
self-image, positive 7
self-perception 10
self-promotion 8–9
self-talk 22
self-trust 14–15, 16, 21–22, 60–61,
      109
shame 62, 72
shit shield 22
'should'ing 118

showing up 61
signature strengths 93
Singapore, MW's life in 85, 159–
      160, 171–174, 186
sisterhood 118–19
social media 161
small, playing 43
spirituality 83; *see also* faith
— defined 140–141
— heath and 141–142
stand-up comedy, trying 5–6
start, permission to 11–12
strength(s)
— capacity for life 86
— empowerment 82–83
— exercise 77–78, 80–81
— habits 80–81, 84–85
— inner sage 88–89
— intuition 86
— journaling 86–87
— overwhelm, feeling of 81–82,
      86
— owning your 103
— self-fullness 79–80
— signature strengths 93
— strengthening your wings
      77–89
— using your 93, 94–95, 130–132
strengths-based workplaces 94
stress 4, 16, 47, 66, 78, 81, 94, 142,
      184, 185, 189, 195
struggle, embracing *see* resistance,
      surrendering
struggle, sharing the 160–161
support, providing 155–157, 165,
      166, 167

Teflon 66, 105
Ten Commandments of Courage
    114–120
thriving 45–46, 95
    — five questions for 70–71
transformation *see* resistance,
    surrendering
trust *see* self-trust
tsunami, Asian Boxing Day 190

uncertainty 133, 149, 165, 173,
    183, 190
    — embracing 184–186
    — neuroscience and 183–184
unlived life 99
uplift, finding 153–169
uplift, people who provide 153–
    169; *see also* connecting

velcro 65–66, 105
vision for your life 37–54
    — executing 44
    — parents' influence 39, 40
    — power and 51, 191–192,
      200–201
    — and values 191–192,
      200–201
vulnerability 59, 74, 160
    — hangover 161–162
    — men and 123, 126–129, 132,
      134
    — power of 132
    — risk and 127–129

weakness(es) 3, 93,
    128–129

Weinstein, Harvey 123
wellbeing 93, 141–142
Williamson, Marianne 102–103,
    192, 199
winging it 115
wings, strengthening your *see*
    strength(s)
women, overcoming challenges
    107–121
    — ambition 111, 113
    — amplifying sisterhood 118–
      119
    — apologising 117
    — barriers and bias against 108
    — beauty, dealing with
      119–120
    — compliments, accepting 115
    — difference, embracing 115–116
    — equal partners 109–110
    — gender confidence gap 110–
      111
    — gender norms 112, 125–127
    — help, asking for 116–117
    — management 114
    — motherhood and career
      113–114
    — nice, being 114–115
    — opportunities, seeking 117
    — power 110
    — role models 113
    — self-belief 112
    — self-criticism 107–109
    — self-deprecation 115,
      102–103
    — self-trust 109
    — 'should'ing 118

— 10 Commandments of courage
   114–120
— winging it 115
— workforce design and 112–113
words, power of 193–195
— 7 ways to harness 194–195

workforce design and women
   112–113
work worth doing 42, 44–45, 200
writer, MW's work as a
   102–103, 110,
   155–157, 173

LET'S STAY CONNECTED!

If this book has inspired you, I'd love to connect and continue supporting you in pursuing your own 'hero's journey' ahead with greater clarity, confidence and courage.

YOU'VE GOT THIS! PODCAST SERIES

I've created a special *You've Got This!* series on my Live Brave podcast where I share how you can apply the principles in this book in your life along with other insights and interviews with extraordinary people, including Marianne Williamson, Tal Ben-Shahar and Rosie Batty.

www.thelivebravepodcast.com

SOCIAL MEDIA

I'd love to be part of your 'online network' and keep inspiring you with my latest videos, insights and event updates.

LIVE BRAVELY NEWSLETTER

If you'd value a regular dose of encouragement, subscribe to my *Live Bravely* newsletter which goes out to people in 50+ countries. It includes updates on my public Live Brave Weekends and other programs in my newsletter (though I promise never to spam you!).

Sign up at **www.margiewarrell.com**

SPEAKING & LEADERSHIP PROGRAMS

I've spoken to thousands of audiences around the world — including organisations such as Google, Deloitte, Johnson & Johnson and SAP — helping people unlock their power as change-makers, thrive through change and fulfil their potential — in work, leadership and life.

Learn more, watch videos and read reviews at **www.margiewarrell.com/speaking**

MEDIA & INTERVIEWS

While I never became a foreign correspondent, I love sharing my expertise through media such *The Today Show, Fox & Friends*, CNN and Bloomberg and many publications and podcasts.

For press kit and media enquiries, visit **www.margiewarrell.com/media**

READ MORE FROM MARGIE

If you enjoyed this book, check out Margie's other books which include the titles below.

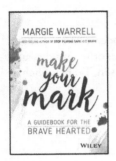

MAKE YOUR MARK
A guidebook to get unstuck and on track to your biggest life.

Your 7-step roadmap to help you make the changes you've been putting off and get 'on purpose' to make your unique mark with greater clarity, confidence and courage. To be read with a pen in hand!

BRAVE
Fifty uplifting chapters with practical strategies to build your bravery and thrive in work, love and life.

Written for busy people, this book is for busy people looking for a regular shot of inspiration, the 50 easy-to-read chapters will inspire you to 'train the brave' in every area of your life.

This book has also been released as *Train the Brave* as part of Wiley's *Be Your Best* series.

STOP PLAYING SAFE
A roadmap for taking the smart risks required to excel in your career, leadership and life.

For career-minded professionals, this book will help you rethink risk, find your Why and make the bold moves needed to enjoy more success at work. Includes insights from Margie's work with trailblazing leaders and entrepreneurs from around the world.